HAMPSTEAD HEATH
KENWOOD EXTENSION

SCALE OF FEET

-Reference-
- KENWOOD 1st Purchase
- KENWOOD 2nd Purchase
- Subsold, restricted from building
- Allotments
- HAMPSTEAD HEATH

C000220286

HIGHGATE

FITZROY PARK

WOOD ESTATE

NIGHTINGALE LANE

Ken Wood

Golf Course

Golf Course

Highgate Ponds

BROOKFIELD

PARLIAMENT HILL

B.G.1 WARD

NORTH

This Plan is based upon the Ordnance Survey by permission of the Ministry of Agriculture and Fisheries and the Controller of H. M. Stationery

STEAD

THE SAVING OF KENWOOD
AND
THE NORTHERN HEIGHTS

*With all good wishes &
admiration to Peter & Ruth*

John Carswell

29 May 92

Also by John Carswell:

The Prospector
The Old Cause
The South Sea Bubble
The Descent on England
English Society 1688–1776
Lives and Letters
The Exile
Government & The Universities in Great Britain
The Porcupine: a Life of Algernon Sidney

THE SAVING OF KENWOOD
AND
THE NORTHERN HEIGHTS

John Carswell

AIDAN ELLIS

First published in the United Kingdom by
Aidan Ellis Publishing, Cobb House, Nuffield,
Henley-on-Thames, Oxon RG9 5RT

First editon 1992

A CIP catalogue record for this book is available
from the British Library

Filmset in Times by Contour Typesetters, Southall, Middx UB2 4BD
Printed in England by Biddles Ltd, Guildford, Surrey GU1 1DA

ISBN 0 85628 208 1

To my father Donald,
who introduced me to Kenwood
but never wrote his projected biography
of the first Earl of Mansfield

CONTENTS

Illustrations

Endpapers: How the Kenwood Estate Fell to the Public
(Hatching shows the estate as it was before purchases
began: heavier hatching the portion finally bought by Lord
Iveagh. Unhatched portions within the black line show the
growth of the Heath apart from the Kenwood Estate.) The
map below is Lawrence Chubb's map for the Kenwood
Preservation Council.

his in
eally the
a pdion
a Plate

The March of the Guards to Finchley by Hogarth
(Courtesy of the Thomas Coram Foundation for Children)

J.C. 2 *William Murray, First Earl of Mansfield,* aged 74, by Joseph
Nollekens
(Courtesy of English Heritage, Iveagh Bequest)

3 The Bank Quay Soapworks in 1886
(Courtesy of Warrington Public Library)

4 Arthur Crosfield, aged 41, when he entered Parliament
(Courtesy of Warrington Public Library)

5 The Mansfield Estate from 'Witanhurst'
(Courtesy of Miss Kathleen Smith)

Preface

My first interest in Kenwood goes back well over sixty years, when as a Hampstead child playing with friends on the East Heath we ranged further than usual and found our way over the palisades of the South Wood into a forest with a kind of fairy palace beyond its mysterious lakes. I asked my father about it, and his vague answers gave me the impression that somewhere there lurked an unsatisfactory story. In fact he must have known a good deal about it, since he was a journalist, a barrister, a biographer, and a Scotsman; and as a result was contemplating a biography of the first Lord Mansfield. It is a pity he abandoned the idea, because it would not only have suited his talents but filled a gap which had been empty for the three-quarters of a century since Lord Campbell covered the ground in his collective *Lives of the Lord Chief Justices* – a work which, as one of them later remarked, 'added a new terror to death'.

But I never tried to explore the black hole this conversation opened in my infant mind until much later, even though other work on the British eighteenth century suggested to me that Lord Mansfield's influence in that world went far beyond his importance as a lawgiver. The final stimulus this time was a renewed interest in the history of the Heath, and therefore of Kenwood and the way it passed into public ownership, and on every side I encountered what seemed to be the received opinion that public ownership of that part of Hampstead Heath was to be mainly attributed to the intervention and generosity of Lord Iveagh.

My inquiries first suggested and then confirmed that no such view is justified, since it ignores the long and painful campaign of the Kenwood Preservation Council and its leader, Arthur Crosfield. That campaign, funded in ways which most of us would find surprising, saved two-thirds of the remaining Mansfield Estate, and there can be little doubt that without its success Lord Iveagh would not have been stimulated to buy the rest. Indeed there is evidence to show that in the final stages Crosfield and Iveagh were acting in concert.

I most gratefully acknowledge help from many quarters in my research for this book. The present Earl of Mansfield generously permitted me a free run of his remarkable family archives, and Mrs Jean Auld, archivist of Dundee University, spared no kindness and trouble to make my choices from that archive accessible to me. A particular debt of gratitude is owed to Dr Peter Barber, of the British Library, who drew my attention to the dramatic estates policy of the first Earl of Mansfield, which not only enlarges our understanding of that great man's contribution to the preservation of the Northern Heights, but sheds a shaft of light over the whole history of them.

Occasionally research brings a new friendship, and it is in this spirit that I mention the great debt I owe to Miss Kathleen Smith, whose recollections of Arthur and Domini Crosfield, for whom she worked as private secretary, have been invaluable. She has provided evidence that only an eye-witness can give, and several of the illustrations in this book. Without her testimony it would have been impossible to present a rounded portrait of Arthur Crosfield. In the same vein, good fortune introduced me to the family historian of the Crosfields, Mr John Fothergill Crosfield, whose impressive history of the widespread family, and other kindnesses, have been indispensable.

Sir Nicholas Goodison's grandfather served as Treasurer of the Kenwood Preservation Council and is commemorated by the fountain between the South Wood and the Highgate Ponds which must mark the middle of the Grand Duke's fairway. Sir Nicholas has kindly provided me with useful information from his grandfather's papers, including one of my illustrations. Lord Moyne has also provided me with interesting insights about his grandfather, the first Lord Iveagh at Kenwood. Sir John Summerson has kindly given me his valuable time on questions concerning the landscape of Kenwood.

That recognised authority on the Heath's (and now Hampstead Garden Suburb's) history, Mr C W Ikin, has been generous in sharing his scholarship with me, and commenting from his legal knowledge on my account of the Iveagh Bequest Act – that riddle of the Statute Book. I also owe to him his clarifying diagram of the way the Heath Mosaic was created, which forms one of my illusrations.

The London Library, the British Library, the Greater London Record office, the Local History Section of the Camden Library at Swiss Cottage, have been the bricks they always are: but I should recall three other librarians to whom I owe special thanks – Mr Rogers, of the Warrington Public Library, whose interest has provided much information and two of my illustrations; Mrs Gosling, and the Highgate Literary and Scientific Institution for access to most interesting documents and an important illustration; and Mrs Stanniforth of Unilever plc for her efforts in giving me access to Lord Leverhulme's letterbooks. I am also grateful to the London Transport Museum, The Thomas Coram Foundation for Children, and to English Heritage for permission to reproduce two of my illustrations.

And last encouragement, for which many thanks are due: to my colleagues of the Heath and Old Hampstead Society; to my wife, who has saved me from obscurities and infelicities, and Inge Goodwin who read several acres of the *Hampstead and Highgate Express*, read each chapter patiently, and pointed out that a young lady in one of my illustrations was not 'enfranchised' but 'emancipated'.

JC
Hampstead 22 September 1991

Prologue

Kenwood and the Murrays

This book is about a famous landscape and two men, widely separated in time, who loved it. One, William Murray first Earl of Mansfield, saw its possibilities, and made it his home and the memorial to his achievements. For more than a century and a half, undamaged by London's expanding urbanisation, it remained in the hands of his heirs down to the fifth generation when surrender to the tide of bricks and mortar seemed almost inevitable. The other man, Arthur Crosfield, then came forward and, against almost overwhelming odds, led the campaign that rescued Kenwood and saved what he always called 'The Northern Heights' to complete the great green tract of public open space with a character which no other great city in the world can boast within five miles of its very centre. No planner would have created it, or even thought of it. It is an accident of history, the fruit of many large and small campaigns, of which the struggle for Kenwood is among the most notable – not least because it was won without spending a penny of government money.

'The Northern Heights' are the ridge connecting Hampstead and Highgate, with Kenwood House between the two, and almost at the summit. You can see it and its scenic importance to the whole London landscape in Hogarth's famous picture *The March of the Guards to Finchley* painted in 1751. The artist set up his easel on what was then the edge of built-up London, where Tottenham Court Road (you can see the sign-board proclaiming the 'Tottenham Court Nurseries' on the left of the picture) meets the then 'New' but now Euston Road. The foreground is taken up with an uproarious departure scene as soldiers, most of them drunk, prepare to march northwards to fight the Jacobite rebels and take leave of a crowd of loose women, beggars, raga-muffins and pickpockets. Beyond, in the middle distance, files with shouldered muskets are trudging already towards an isolated little group of buildings set in open country – Chalk Farm. In the far distance Hogarth, almost like a renaissance painter looking through the window beside his sitter, has delicately touched in 'The Northern Heights' themselves, with the townlet of Hampstead on the left. Moving the eye to the right (or east) one can make out first the lonely Spaniards' Inn, and then the group of buildings that formed Kenwood House when William Murray bought it and the surrounding ground four years after the picture was painted. All the rest is open land.

When William Murray bought the place in 1754 it was not a particularly important estate: the brick mansion, with its front door almost on the main road between Hampstead and Highgate (as it then ran) was some sixty years old. The back windows commanded a large sloping sward which ended in a chain of marshy ponds and then a wood, whose southern boundary marked the limit of the estate.* But the view southward towards London was remarkable. Since the Union with Scotland the property had provided a convenient London residence for a series of Scottish grandees whose real homes and power lay north of the Border, and for a time one of them even let it to his banker. William Murray bought it from the last of these, the Earl of Bute, later Prime Minister.

Murray was an exceptional man, and but for the total destruction of all his personal papers (in a way to be later described) would be recognised far more fully as one of the greatest public men of his age. When Boswell claimed him as a Scot whose abilities reached the highest English standards even Johnson made the grudging admission that 'much may be made of a Scotsman – if he be caught young'. And it is true that his education was entirely English. From the time he left the family home in Perthshire as a boy he never, so far as is known, set foot in Scotland again in his whole long life, which began on 2 March 1705.

---

* The terminology of Kenwood is confusing. This wood is often thought of, and spoken of, as 'Ken Wood', but for clarity I shall refer to it throughout as 'The South Wood', reserving the term 'Kenwood' for the whole estate, whatever its boundaries at different times, and 'Kenwood House' for the mansion on it.

He was self-made, though of aristocratic birth. His early poverty may have been exaggerated, but he was a younger son in a family of eight children in which the expectations of even the eldest were limited to the small estate depending on the grandly named but sadly dilapidated Scone Palace which had been conferred, along with the title of Viscount Stormont, on his ancestor by King James VI in 1600 for unspecified services in the mysterious affair of the Gowrie Conspiracy.

Shortage of money was not the only handicap William Murray had to contend with in Hanoverian England. His family were, and always had been, supporters of the banished House of Stuart and Jacobite sympathisers. All his life he was publicly smeared with this association, even to the point of being denounced as a Roman Catholic, perhaps a Jesuit. Nevertheless, after an early education at the local school in Perth, he made his way to that nursery of eighteenth-century talent, Westminister, by the influence of the then influential Tory Dean of Westminister, Francis Atterbury, where he made a number of useful friends, through one of whom he was later introduced to Alexander Pope, whose life-long intimate and admirer he became. Pope became so devoted to Murray – seventeen years his junior – that he insisted, almost from his deathbed, on visiting his friend once more, and made him his executor.

By then Murray's career had advanced with astonishing speed. After Christ Church Oxford he qualified as a barrister, and long before he was forty

8

reached the top of his profession. Among his clients were the great Duchess of Marlborough, the Corporation of Edinburgh, whose charter he rescued from forfeiture after the Porteous riots, and the celebrated Captain Jenkins, whose lost ear precipitated war with Spain and the fall of Walpole. But his most influential client of all was the great whig organiser, the Duke of Newcastle, whose private legal and financial adviser he became. In 1741, when he was thirty-six, Newcastle brought him into Parliament for Boroughbridge and put him in charge of organising the government's business in the House of Commons.

This was in the same year as his almost exact contemporary William Pitt. They began as rivals and went on to be irreconcilable enemies. Murray was cool, analytic, persuasive, almost at times too sane; Pitt was heroic, instinctive, theatrical, occasionally mad. Murray never forgave Pitt his immense popularity and triumphant premiership.

In 1742, when he was just thirty-seven, Murray became Solicitor-General as well as leader of the Commons, and soon found himself sending the defeated Jacobite peers of the '45 – some of them old friends of his family – to the scaffold. He did it fairly, but without hesitation. In 1754, the year he bought Kenwood, he was advanced, again by the Duke of Newcastle, to be Attorney-General. Two years later, he claimed the traditional right to succeed to a vacancy in the highest judicial office, Lord Chief Justice. He was forty-nine.

There can be little doubt this post had always been

9

his aim in life. The Duke of Newcastle sent the most pathetic appeals, imploring him to stay in the Commons, and joined them with vast offers of pensions and sinecures. When they were refused he tried threats. He would withhold the peerage that always went with the post. The reply from Murray was that in that case he would still leave the House of Commons, and earn his living at the bar. The Duke gave in, and Murray became Baron Mansfield and Lord Chief Justice.

During the thirty-two years he held that office – an unrivalled period – he became one of the greatest judges ever to sit on the English bench. But his influence extended far beyond that. He sat in many cabinets; twice it was suggested he should be Prime Minister; three times he refused to be Lord Chancellor; he took a stand on major political issues, such as American Independence, of which he was a fierce opponent. And yet, as a judge, he showed complete indifference to political opinion.

He was rich even before he bought Kenwood, and from the first intended it to be the symbol of his membership of the landed oligarchy to which his talents had raised him. He had a house in Bloomsbury as a base from which to work, but Kenwood became his passion, and to fulfil it he called on the most distinguished and fashionable designers of his age, the brothers Robert and James Adam. They began embellishing Kenwood six years after Mansfield bought it, and their work continued for fifteen years, designing, building, landscaping and furnishing. The original brickwork was covered with stucco, the height was raised by a storey, and a new wing, one of Robert Adam's greatest achievements, was added on the east to form a library, balancing the existing orangery to the west. Mansfield himself had seen the immense possibilities of the southward view on London, and the library windows took full advantage of it.

At Kenwood he was able to receive on terms of equality the noble landowners of the world in which he now moved. He did so with the greater confidence because many of the greatest of them owed him large sums on mortages. Among these were two who became Prime Ministers – the Duke of Portland and the Marquess of Rockingham, whose loans together came to nearly £30,000. Lord Fitzwilliam, Rockingham's heir, was mortgaged to Mansfield for £21,000; the Duke of Rutland for £6,000. Altogether the capital he owned in mortgages came to £111,000, yielding an income of nearly £5,000 a year. Here, undoubtedly, lay an important element of his immense influence. And if one adds a sum nearly twice as large invested in other securities, he was, in our terms, a millionaire many times over.

For Lord Mansfield the southward view was the most important feature of Kenwood, and to protect it from what he could even then foresee as the threat of creeping urbanisation he bought land there whenever he could, so that by the time of his death he owned the slope as far as Gospel Oak, where his boundary is still commemorated by Mansfield Road. Parliament Hill Fields were his, and so was much land to the east, adjoining Fitzroy Park. He did not look for income from these purchases, which were protective.

But northward, beyond Hampstead Lane, his grand design took a different form. Here too he had a long-term scenic intention, but the main motive was financial. His neighbour to the north was the Bishop of London, from whom he systematically acquired leases covering some seven hundred acres of grain, pasture, and timber – they included Highgate Woods. Their large rent roll could be used to sustain the scenically important but unproductive land to the south and make the estate the self-supporting entity he intended for his heirs.

This policy of investment began during the years he was employing Adam, and duly brought more than a thousand acres under his control – leasehold to the north, freehold to the south and west – stretching from Gospel Oak to Hornsey, with Kenwood House at its centre.

The expansion across Hampstead Lane also had in mind the removal of the Lane itself to a proper distance from the front of the house which was within twenty yards or so of the traffic, and over-looked by a mound beyond it. So much can be guessed from the addition of the massive portico on the north front of the house, which must have looked very lonely without the wings that were added within a few months of Mansfield's death by his successor. However, there is documentary proof that the whole concept of the grander northern approach belonged to the first Earl's time. It is in the shape of an endorsement by the second Earl of a letter from the

Bishop of London giving his agreement to move the
Lane and, in consequence, bring a substantial strip
of land leased from the Bishop into the Mansfield
Estate, and form the North Wood. The Bishop's
letter is dated 15 July 1793, and the second Earl's
endorsement reads:

> Addressed to David, Second Earl of Mansfield.
> Lord Mansfield died 20 March 1793 and the first
> improvement which had always been contemp-
> lated but very properly deferred by Lord
> Mansfield, who would have been put to incon-
> venience, was the moving (of) the road.

This also provides the context for the enquiries
made by the second Earl (then still Lord Stormont)
as early as 1791 for suitable landscapers. The new
land for the scheme would be no more than open
woodland, and would have to become park. Indeed,
such enquiries on his own initiative as heir, without
the approval of his uncle and benefactor, would have
been regarded as almost indecent.*

§

During the thirty-nine years between buying

---

* The old line of Hampstead Lane has survived down to the
time of writing this as a Parish, Borough and Police boundary.
Only now is consideration being given for administration to
follow what Lord Mansfield did nearly two centuries ago for his
own convenience. The Bishop of London's letter is in the
Mansfield papers. Bundle 578.

Kenwood and his death, the great Earl of Mansfield lived two distinct lives. One was that of the triumphant landed oligarch to which he had raised himself. As such he was profoundly conservative, hostile to all change, an opponent of both the American and French Revolutions, which he lived to see. But during more than three decades in which he sat as Lord Chief Justice he set himself the task of sweeping away the traditional obstacles and prejudice in the law which offended his common sense and perception of utility. Bentham is said to have lurked in the undergrowth of Kenwood in the hope of seeing his ideal judge, and repeatedly mentions him with homage in his works. A stream of modernising judgment flowed from him throughout his judicial career, with hardly any department untouched.

He reformed the law of insurance and the law of evidence, sweeping away the absurd rule that a credible witness had to be a Christian. He virtually invented commercial law. He intervened to protect a Jew who was being offensively cross-examined about his means to stand bail for a co-religionist. He found in favour of a local authority sued by the ratepayers for providing a maternity ward for pauper mothers, saying he had never heard it was contrary to law to deliver children. Constant war was waged in his court against procedural and technical devices to delay decisions and he horrified his colleagues by insisting (though in this he was outvoted) that if there was evidence of what the writer of a document had really meant, his intention should not be frustrated by his inadvertently having used a

14

technical expression which meant something else to
professional lawyers.

In dealing with crime he was not (as is sometimes
suggested) a harsh judge. 'Tenderness,' he said, in a
case he heard almost at the end of his career, 'ought
always to prevail in criminal cases. So that, at least,
to take care that a man may not suffer otherwise than
by due cause of law; nor have any hardship done
him, or severity exercised upon him when the
construction may admit of reasonable doubt or
difficulty.' He showed this in practice by intervening
in the case of a man charged with the capital offence
of stealing a trinket valued at more than forty
shillings by demanding to see the object and ruling it
was worth less. 'Under forty shillings, my Lord!'
shouted the furious owner. 'Why the fashion [work-
manship] alone cost me more than double the sum!'
Mansfield turned to the jury with the words 'God
forbid, gentlemen, we should hang a man for
fashion's sake' and directed an acquittal. His assize
notebooks show numerous reminders to recommend
reprieves in cases where the law had compelled him
to pass a death sentence.

But Mansfield's most celebrated case concerned
what today we should call human rights. Granville
Sharpe, one of the earliest and greatest anti-slavery
campaigners, managed to get James Somersett, a
West Indian slave who had escaped from his master
on a visit to England and been recaptured, produced
on *Habeas Corpus*. The master pleaded he would
have been protected by the laws of Jamaica, a British
possession. It was not only a difficult case, with

precedents pointing either way, but a test of the status of several thousand slaves estimated to be in England at that time, and there are strong signs Mansfield did not want to settle such a case at all. It does the more credit to him that despite his instinctive conservatism he freed Somersett:

> 'The state of slavery,' he said, 'is of such a nature, that it is incapable of being introduced on any reasons, moral or political, but only on positive law . . . It is so odious that nothing can be suffered to support it but positive law . . . I cannot say this case is allowed by the law of England; and therefore the black must be discharged.'

This judgment legally enfranchised about fifteen thousand slaves then living in England. It did not, of course, abolish slavery in British Colonies or put an end to the slave trade, which continued to flourish. But it was the first, and a well-publicised step on the long road to abolition.*

---

* It is worth noting that Mansfield had a personal interest in the slave question in his dependent Dido, who was the illegitimate daughter of a naval nephew of his and a Jamaican slave mother. He took over her education and treated her as one of the family at Kenwood, where visitors were surprised to see her take her place at table for dinner. She appears with the Earl's two devoted nieces in a picture by Zoffany, now at Scone Palace. He provided her with an adequate income of her own in his will, in which he was careful to insert words to remove any attempt to claim she was a slave.

Intellect and rationalism were Mansfield's out-
standing qualities as a judge, but these qualities do
not make a man popular, and he was one of the most
hated men of his time. Its two greatest journalists,
Wilkes and 'Junius' created a brilliant image of him
as a self-seeking Scotsman, a crypto-Jacobite,
probably a secret Roman Catholic whose aim was to
subvert Church and Constitution, and it percolated
far below the educated classes. The resentment of
ordinary people was confirmed by two cases in which
Mansfield set his face against religious disability.

The first concerned a Protestant Dissenter, the
second a Roman Catholic.

For many years the City of London had collected
involuntary contributions towards building the
Mansion House from dissenting members of the
Corporation. They could not act as sheriffs because
they could not conscientiously take the prescribed
Anglican oaths, but were elected just the same, and
then heavily fined under a City by-law for refusing to
serve. A test case on the legality of this was brought
by the dissenting lobby, and Mansfield's opinion was
delivered in the House of Lords, to become embedded
in English law. The practice, he held, was contrary to
natural justice:

'It cannot be shown from the principles of
natural or revealed religion that, independent of
positive law, temporal punishments ought to be
inflicted for mere opinions with respect to
modes of worship. Persecutions for sincere,
though erroneous conscience is not to be

deduced from reason or the fitness of things . . .
Conscience is not controllable by human laws,
nor amenable to human tribunals. Persecution,
or attempts to force conscience will never
produce conviction, and are only calculated to
make hypocrites and martyrs.'

The other case concerned a supposed (and almost
certainly actual) Roman Catholic priest charged
with the serious offence under a seventeenth-century
statute of saying Mass. The evidence was that of an
informer, and the penalty was life imprisonment. In
his summing up Mansfield pointed out that no
evidence had been produced to show that the
accused was in holy orders, and such proof was
indispensable for a conviction. He therefore directed
an acquittal. Soon afterwards Parliament passed an
Act abolishing the offence of saying Mass.

This step in the relief of Catholic disabilities
fuelled the anti-Catholic agitation and ferocious
mob violence which broke out in the summer of 1780
under the leadership of the anti-Catholic demagogue
Lord George Gordon. Mansfield's house in Bloomsbury was one of the main targets, and was burned to
the ground, along with its contents, its famous
library, and all Mansfield's papers, the accumulation
of a distinguished lifetime. He narrowly escaped the
mob himself, and fled under the protection of his
nephew Lord Stormont to Kenwood, where he was
greeted by the still empty shelves of the magnificent
library that Adam had finished only a year earlier.
Soon afterwards he was asked to contribute his legal

opinion to the House of Lords in a debate about the legality of the measures taken to suppress the riots. 'I have not consulted my books. I have no books,' he said.

The violence (he held) was a rebellion which all citizens, whether their coats were red or brown, had a duty to suppress by all force at their disposal. No criticism of the soldiers could be made. He declined all compensation for his losses, though it was offered, saying it was his own fault for ordering the soldiers sent to protect him into a remote side street for fear of provoking the mob.

After that he rarely left Kenwood, though he remained Lord Chief Justice for another eight years, when he retired at the age of eighty-three. Kenwood became in every sense his home, and during the five years of his retirement he never slept away from it.

During those last years he delighted in showing its beauties to visitors, and spent much time and money on its care. The 'sham bridge' belongs to this time, as does the redefinition of the ponds to give the impression of a single sheet of water flowing under it and descending in imagination downhill towards London. With his own hands he planted cedars on the fringe of the South Wood and the last of them, by then more than a hundred feet high, survived more than a century before being felled as dangerous in 1909, when the decision to part with his treasure had already been taken.

This great man was childless, though happily married. He therefore had to choose an heir, and found one in the senior living representative of his own family, David, seventh Viscount Stormont, his elder brother's son. This decision was to be of very great importance for the whole future of Kenwood because it placed the estate in possession of a family whose main interests and affections lay far away in Perthshire. Lord Stormont himself directed his heart should lie in his ancestral home of Scone, and of the six Earls of Mansfield who successively owned Kenwood only one, the first, died there. None were born there. Though it was carefully protected, it declined over five generations into a secondary residence, not neglected, but little lived in, frozen as it were in time.

The seventh Viscount Stormont was only twenty years younger than his famous uncle, and owed him much, not only in expectation but for a successful political and diplomatic career. He was in turn British Representative in Dresden, Vienna and Paris, and sat in the cabinets of Lord North and the Younger Pitt. An immense archive shows him to have been industrious, well-informed and cultivated. He had travelled widely, and met many of the most distinguished Europeans of his time. As a young man he had exchanged verses with the Italian poet Metastasio, and the great antiquarian Winckelmann paid him the rather barbed compliment of describing his classical knowledge as exceptional for a man of such high rank. Among his friends were Necker, Louis XVI's reforming minister, his charming and talented wife, and their remarkable daughter, Madame de Stael.

Some people found him haughty and overbearing,

20

and he was criticised for parsimony. Nor was he an easy master. 'I trust your Lordship would agree,' wrote one infuriated steward on his Scottish estates, 'that I have never been wanting in proper respect for my superiors in rank, or especially my employer, *but I am not a vassal*!'

The Lord Chief Justice went to immense trouble to ensure that not only his estate but his title should descend to his nephew's line. When Lord North raised him to an earldom in 1776 he extracted the exceptional provision that it should go to his nephew's *wife* because he was under the impression that Stormont himself, as a Scottish peer, could not inherit a title created since the Union. But when, only a year or two before his death, a judgment of the House of Lords showed that in this at least the great lawyer had been wrong, he exercised his immense influence to get the extraordinary privilege of a *second* earldom, which would descend this time direct to his nephew. As a result Stormont and his wife became Earl and Countess of Mansfield in their own separate rights, and transmitted to their descendants the remarkable title of Earls of Mansfield and Mansfield. As part of the arrangement Lord Stormont's vote in the House of Lords was permanently put at the disposal of the government.

But in one respect the first Earl did not comply with the habits of the noble landowners of his world. He created no entail, but deliberately left his heirs to do what they pleased with the estate. In his will, made in 1782, he wrote that his estate went

21

'to those who are nearest and dearest to me' who would care for it 'according to events and contingencies which it is impossible for me to foresee, or trace through the many labyrinths of time and chance'.

Indeed the words of a great mind. They seem to have been respected by successive generations of his heirs,* and had the effect of freeing them from the obstacles which confronted their neighbours, the Maryon Wilsons, in developing their estate.

§

No heir could have been more devoted to his predecessor's memory than the new Earl. He not only commissioned the massive monument by Flaxman which commemorates the first Lord Mansfield in Westminster Abbey,** but populated Kenwood House with recollections of him: a bronze bust by Nollekens, a miniature by Birch, a portrait gem in James Tassie's vitreous paste. And he at once

* There are signs of a period of entail between 1860 and 1899. But even this did not prevent the development of the southern part of the estate beside Parliament Hill or the sales to the public in 1889. Certainly from 1899 onwards the Earls were under no restraint about development or sale.
** It is based on the well-known portrait by Reynolds, with the great man in full glory sitting on the bench. The second Earl disliked Flaxman's first sketch, especially the wig, 'which is certainly calculated to strike terror into either the patron of art or the artist'. (M. Box 18, 11 September 1793)

put in hand the extensive works his uncle had approved for the northern aspect of the house. The architect, Robert Nasmith, seems also to have been appointed by the first Earl, and when he died in the summer of 1793 the new Earl gruffly rejected Humphry Repton's suggestion that the place should be filled by his friend Mr Wilkins, and appointed the existing surveyor, George Saunders, with the brief comment, 'He is well acquainted with the plans.'

There is no convincing evidence that the second Earl's activities extended to the southern view from the house, which the first Earl had himself so recently improved substantially and survives today. His main contribution was the two rather undistinguished wings in whitish brick which we now see, and the creation of an approach through the new North Wood, for which he consulted two designers, Eames and the celebrated Humphry Repton.

Both are mentioned among the names the second Earl collected from his friends before succeeding to the estate, and Eames is shown as having spent one day at Kenwood in the voluminous accounts of the improvements which the Earl carefully audited each month. Repton certainly also came to Kenwood in the early summer of 1793, and sent in a 'memorandum' together with an account for which he sought settlement to avoid having 'to ask a favour of my bankers'. This letter preceded, by three days, severe instructions about the new works issued by the Earl in preparation for an absence of several months. It begins:

Directions respecting the order in which my works are to be carried out in my absence. I am fully determined to push the works on with vigour and in the most methodical manner.*

But it contains no reference to landscaping.

The earliest clear indication of the new northern approach is a sketch dated 2/3 July 1794 showing 'Mr Townley's Plan with Mr Elkington's notes' on the important subject of drainage. On the new line of Hampstead Lane is a new octagonal lodge leading to a drive which swings in a single curve of 'about 200 yards' towards the house**. A wood is shown to the east but not to the west of the drive. The evidence is fragmentary and uncertain but we can be sure the whole of Kenwood House and its surroundings, as we have inherited them, are not very far from the first Earl of Mansfield's overall wishes.

§

* 7 August 1793, M. Box 112. Whether the 'memorandum' sent by Repton was in fact one of Repton's 'Red Books' is unclear but there certainly was a 'Red Book'. It is referred to in correspondence between Repton and the second Earl's executors and paid for, but does not survive, and is not referred to in any of Repton's own lists of these celebrated productions. His own MS autobiography does not refer to any commission at Kenwood. The record shows him as paying, at most, three brief visits spread over three years of intense activity on other commissions. On the rather fragmentary evidence I follow Sir John Summerson's view that any influence of Repton should be sought in the area north of the House.
** M. Bundle 258

The second Earl's reign, though active, was brief, and lasted only three years; but those of his son and grandson covered more than a century. Both were resolute enemies of change in any form, and saw it as their duty to keep Kenwood substantially as it had come down to them, even though it was not their home, and they spent less and less time there. Their Kenwood steward Mr Edward Hunter had been appointed in the first Earl's time, and was as conservative as his last master, the third Earl, who defied his own party leaders in voting with the die-hard Tory peers against the Reform Bill of 1832.

The third Earl applied similar principles to his Hampstead estate. When his neighbour, Sir Thomas Maryon Wilson, asked the House of Lords to pass a bill allowing him to build on contiguous Hampstead Heath in breach of a paternal entail, Lord Mansfield opposed it; and when Sir Thomas complained that scores of similar bills had gone through on the nod he was crushed by the Earl's frankness. It might be hard on Sir Thomas, but those bills did not concern Hampstead. 'I oppose you on private grounds, but I will put it on public ground, and I know I can beat you.' Lord Mansfield then subscribed £50 to the campaign against Maryon Wilson. The scheme was defeated.

This Earl lived to see Queen Victoria crowned, and entertained King William IV and his Queen at Kenwood with eight hundred guests in 1835. But he did not often stay there, for he travelled extensively abroad and spent much of his time in Scone, where he demolished the crumbling home of his ancestors

25

and built a large, but unappealing mansion in its place.

The tradition continued and deepened under the fourth Earl, his son, whose long reign survived the Queen's Diamond Jubilee and made him 'father' of the House of Lords. When he was still the heir and an MP, he was tipped for a promising career in the Conservative Party. But it is unlikely its then leader, Sir Robert Peel, would have encouraged a follower who opposed reform of any kind, almost on principle. On succeeding to the earldom in 1840 the fourth Earl retired to Scotland where, apart from a month or two each year in London, he spent the rest of his long life.

Residence at Scone was by this time not merely a matter of preference for the Earls of Mansfield: it was essential. They were now among the wealthiest proprietors in Scotland, and Scone Palace was the centre of a huge interest covering fifty thousand acres on which stood three major country houses, while underneath were vast quantities of coal. The income from rents and coal royalties was equivalent to two or three million a year in our money. Management and the local power associated with it (the third and fourth Earls were successively Lords Lieutenant of both Clackmannanshire and Fife) claimed much of the proprietor's time and attention, and compared to this responsibility Kenwood was like a remote island possession.*

---

* Opportunities of adding to it were not, however, neglected, and under the fourth Earl the Kenwood Estate reached its greatest extent, by the acquisition of Fitzroy Park to the east (in 1840) and Evergreen Hill to the west (in 1850).

26

Indeed by the late nineteenth century it was almost an island in another sense – a green one – alongside the adjacent green of Hampstead Heath which had been saved for the public in 1879. From the south the tide of bricks and mortar had covered Gospel Oak, South End, and even one slope of Parliament Hill. To the east and west it had climbed the summits of the ridge to engulf Hampstead and Highgate and closed on the further side of the leased lands at Hornsey. The new railway brought cockney trippers to the very boundaries of the park, and displaced wild life found refuge on the Earl's slumbering property. From these long years of salutary neglect the Kenwood lands derive an atmosphere which even now distinguishes them from the rest of the Heath.

Their survival would have been threatened much sooner if it had not been for the self-sustaining system installed by the first Earl, under which the rents from the leased lands paid for the rest of the estate, and the proprietor in Scotland did not have to worry about subsidising an increasingly useless possession. So, as *The Times* reflected in the obituary of the fourth Earl, 'for a period of upwards of a century covered by his father's and his own proprietorship there was continuity of policy'.

But even before the fourth Earl's death this continuity suffered a rude interruption which marks the beginning of the end, though the damage was repaired for a time. In 1885 the energetic Ecclesiastical Commissioners, who had replaced the sleepy administration of the Bishop of London as owners of the lands leased to the Earls of Mansfield, decided to

27

call them in with a view to development. This not only struck at the self-supporting system at Kenwood but brought in question the status of the North Wood, which had been treated as an integral part of the Kenwood Estate for nearly a century. This in turn started ugly rumours that the Earl was himself planning to recover his losses by building on Parliament Hill Fields. A counter-movement was started to add them to the Heath.

The Mansfield family, driven onto the defensive, managed to rescue some remnants of the old policy. The Ecclesiastical Commissioners were persuaded to concede the freehold of the North Wood as compensation for surrender of the other leases, but the century-long control beyond Hampstead Lane was gone for ever, together with the income from it.

To make up the loss of income, a capital sum was raised by selling more than half of the remaining estate to the south – two hundred and sixty-seven acres – to the Metropolitan Board of Works as an addition to the Heath for £309,000. It was a great achievement for the conservation interest, headed at that time by the Duke of Westminster and Lord Eversley, which raised one-third of the price and also so stirred the conscience of the Ecclesiastical Commissioners that they sold Highgate Woods to the City of London Corporation for the benefit of the public.

From the point of view of the Earls of Mansfield the transaction had a double benefit. Not only did the capital inflow provide an income for the two hundred and twenty acres that they retained, but it

28

preserved the view from the ridge for ever, just as effectively as when they owned it themselves.

These changes were accomplished in 1889 and nine years later the aged fourth Earl died and was succeeded by his elder grandson, whose reign provides a brief *fin de siècle* interlude in the history of Kenwood. The fifth Earl was a bachelor, and still much courted, especially as he was still under forty. Though he continued to treat Scone as his home, he liked Kenwood and was often in residence there, becoming a figure in the life of Hampstead and Highgate. In accordance with his family's tradition of support for the Conservatives, he was chairman of the local constituency party, threw the house open at weekends for charitable and political occasions, and took a prominent part in local life generally: President of the Heath Protection Society and the Highgate Literary and Scientific Institute, Patron of the tennis and football clubs. The lights shone once more from the windows of Kenwood House for his frequent entertainments, and he would gladly show visitors the beauties of his grounds. In short he did all that a local nobleman should do, but he died, unmarried and childless in 1906, the year of the general election that brought the axe to the roots of the power of the landed aristocracy.

The new, sixth Earl, the fifth Earl's younger brother, was a clear-headed and realistic man whose entire life centred on Scone and his Scottish estates, which he rarely left, even to go as far as Edinburgh. As for London, his engagement diaries show he visited it only half a dozen times in ten years, and never stayed for more than a week.

He regarded Kenwood as a white elephant, and declined to follow his brother in any of the local positions he had held in Hampstead and Highgate. His stern nature dictated that all positions implied corresponding responsibilities, and he had quite enough of these in Scotland, where he regularly fulfilled all the duties that could be expected of a great proprietor.*

So, very early in his reign, he decided to part with Kenwood and to part with it to the best advantage. Its value as building land had risen greatly in recent years. His decision was strengthened by the arrival of death duties – one of his few journeys to London was to vote against the Budget that imposed them – and the sale of Kenwood would not only eliminate death duties on that estate but bring in funds to defend the Scottish estates when duty inevitably fell on them.

His decision became known in 1910, and the cause of the Heath was at once aroused. From the original ground that had been extracted from the Maryon Wilsons with so much blood and tears it now had several victories behind it and could rely on the support of the press, notably *The Times*. The Heath was now a good deal bigger than the remaining

---

* He was remarkably industrious and systematic. His archives show that in a single day he would dispose of a dozen letters, endorsing the pith of his answer on the back of each. When a manufacturer of dog-food courteously sought his permission to offer his gamekeeper a bottle of whisky as a Christmas box, he carefully replied that he agreed with the proposal but not the principle. 'But since graft is universal, it is best it should be acknowledged, rather than concealed.'

Kenwood Estate. But that estate was still the key to the landscape as a whole, reaching up to the commanding ridge. So far the estate policy of the Mansfield family had served the Heath. Its reversal would ruin all that had so far been achieved in that great cause. That was to be the struggle with which the rest of this book deals.

Only once did the sixth Earl of Mansfield have doubts about his intentions. In the midst of the struggle he wrote to one of the wisest and most respected of the conservative nobility, Lord Lansdowne, asking for his ethical judgment on the decision to sell. We do not have his letter but we can guess what it said from Lansdowne's answer. Yes, it said, 'you are right to sell a property which you no longer feel justified in possessing, to fortify yourself against the storm that is blowing, and will blow harder still.'

The campaigners to save Kenwood and add it to the Heath faced a determined seller, insistent on his price. They would not have succeeded if they had not been led by a man possessing peculiar origins, motives and qualifications.

Arthur Crosfield

Arthur Crosfield and the sixth Earl of Mansfield
were almost exact contemporaries. They were not
only born within a year of each other – the Earl in
1864, Crosfield in 1865 – but entered Parliament in
the same year, 1906; the Earl to the House of Lords
on the death of his brother, Arthur Crosfield to the
Commons as Liberal victor at Warrington Lancs in
the great Liberal landslide of that general election.
Both, by the time that point is reached, were very
wealthy men, but there all resemblance ends.

Crosfield came of a family of grocers, originally
Quakers, whose Westmorland farming ancestors
had been converted in the middle of the seventeenth
century by the preaching of Fox himself. In the
eighteenth century a branch of the Crosfields settled
in Warrington, as wholesale grocers, and in the year
before Waterloo one of them, Joseph,* set up there
at Bank Quay, on the shore of the Mersey, as a soap
manufacturer.

It seems possible that the Crosfields had been
drawn to Warrington originally by the strong

dissenting communities that existed there, as manifested particularly by that pioneering educational institution, the Warrington Academy. It catered for those who were unable to fulfil the religious tests imposed for admission to Oxford and Cambridge, and taught them modern subjects, such as French and science, as well as systematic study of the Bible. There Jean-Paul Marat, then an obscure wandering journalist, taught French for a time, and Priestley, the discoverer of oxygen, taught chemistry. Chemistry was one of Joseph Crosfield's strengths, and he had studied it for six years as apprentice to a Quaker druggist. The seeds of Crosfields as a chemically based firm were planted early.

Thanks to sound Quaker business habits and a knowledge of applied chemistry, Joseph prospered, and by the time of his death in 1844 he was one of the town's leading business men and citizens. Whatever opinions Lord Chief Justice Mansfield may have expressed about religious tolerance, Joseph Crosfield, as a Quaker, still could not serve in any municipal office, but he gave generously towards improving the lot of Warrington's working people, especially their education, and many hundreds of his fellow-townsmen of all denominations followed his funeral.

The firm he left behind him became a cornucopia of industrial possibilities. Soap is a combination of

* There were five brothers. From one is descended the branch associated with Harrison and Crosfield, and with Crosfield Electronics. They intermarried with the Cadburys, and have remained Quakers. The descendants of Joseph, Arthur Crosfield's father, as we shall see, did not.

an acid (which a wide range of animal or vegetable materials will satisfy) and an alkali, normally soda ash (sodium carbonate), which, as Joseph Crosfield had perceived, is easily produced from the Cheshire salt flats only a short distance from Warrington. One of these flats indeed was, oddly enough, owned by Lord Mansfield. Flowing from the process of soap manufacture (but still discarded as waste in Joseph's time) is glycerine, with its multiplicity of uses in medicine, cosmetics, and explosives. Nor, with chemical sophistication and research, did the possibilities end there. Margarine, detergents (Persil, one of Crosfields' patents is still produced in Warrington), cement, hydrogenation of foods, all belong to the family tree of soap manufacture, and long before Brunner, Mond, and Lever entered the celebrated struggle the scientific alignment and energetic management of the Crosfields was making one of the earliest science-based firms in the country, and one of the largest soap manufacturers in the world.

When Joseph Crosfield started in business soap was a luxury, and was heavily taxed. There were resident excisemen in the soapery, as at a distillery, scoring the output for tax, and locking the vats when they went off duty to prevent illicit production. But in 1853 Mr Gladstone, then Chancellor of the Exchequer, abolished the tax on soap, in a fiscal measure that could be said to mark the transition from earlier to later Victorianism. Cheap soap was put within the reach of the masses. The personal grime that pervades the reports of Mayhew and the descriptions of Dickens as a hallmark of the poor,

34

began to give way to the scrubbed ideal of the later part of the century. Cleaner clothes, floors, schools, hospitals steadily improved social life and hygiene. Cleanliness at last came affordably nearer godliness and the sales of soap increased by leaps and bounds. So did the competitiveness of the manufacturers in a rapidly expanding market. The marketing of soap can therefore claim, with patent medicines, to be one of the great progenitors of the advertising industry.

Warrington in the 1860's, was not an attractive place. The best that the author of Murray's Guide could manage, writing when Arthur was five years old, is depressing:

> Though it is situated by no means unpicture-squely on rising ground, on the right bank of the Mersey, which here flows in a series of curves, it has not an inviting aspect; nor is the impression lessened by a nearer inspection, the streets generally being mean, narrow, and very dirty.

The generosity of Arthur's father and grandfather in endowing amenities – public baths, schools, social facilities, public buildings, and the first free library ever opened in England – made little difference to the dingy, smelly, cooped-up surroundings of their business. The Crosfields were considerate employers for their time, offering steady jobs for faithful work, and seasonable help for an employee facing un-deserved difficulty. Nevertheless, and in great measure because of their factory, Warrington was a wretched town. It is not surprising that when Arthur was seven or eight the prosperous Crosfields, now headed by Arthur's father John, moved into a more comfortable house newly built in the green fields of Cheshire.

John Crosfield, Arthur's father, was an extremely decisive man who led the firm to new heights of prosperity during his long reign, which almost reached the end of the century. He also abandoned the rule, though not wholly the principles, of his Quaker forebears by marrying out of the Meeting to an Anglican wife, and adopting her form of worship. In the same vein he decided to send his eldest son, Arthur, to Malvern, a recent additon to the list of public schools, having been founded in the year of Arthur's birth.

The record of Arthur's schooling is peculiar. He threw himself desperately into his work, and in consequence, as he revealed in an extraordinary burst of confidence to the Warrington workforce, he broke down more than once and had to be sent home. He blamed 'eager overwork, foolish overwork, still more foolishly, as I think, encouraged by foolish masters who should have had more sense than to drive the willing horse'. In the end his father moved him to Uppingham, but even at the age of twenty-seven he admitted to not having fully overcome the effect of these nervous breakdowns, and doubted if he ever would.

It speaks a great deal for his determination and abilities that he emerged from his schooling with three natural talents unimpaired: music, poetry and sport. All these recur in his life not just as recreations, but as incentives in his public and private life. He was a competent pianist and violinist, ventured on composition, and was a firm beliver in the civilising value of music. He carried this to the point of advocating free or subsidised public performances. In poetry he was widely read and retentive, and if his prolific verses are not inspired in the highest sense, they are correct and euphonious and have themes on which he felt strongly. Not many men have written a poem about sulphuric acid.* In sport he excelled, especially at games requiring a good eye: tennis, fives, billiards, but, above all, golf, in which he was to reach championship standard. Many of his friendships were based on golf, and the Kenwood story would not have fallen quite as it did if its leading figure had not been a passionate and respected golfer.

It is not surprising that a man of this origin and temperament was a lover of the countryside and the wild open air, a walker and climber. As with music, this enthusiasm was governed by the civic conscience he had inherited towards broadening opportunity for its enjoyment by the kind of people he saw all round him in the mean streets of Warrington.

All this is clear in the extraordinary speech he gave to the workforce of Joseph Crosfield and Sons at their annual gala in 1892. It covered almost every topic and must have taken at least an hour to deliver. He makes no bones about his laissez-faire economics, his hostility to socialism, and the need for profits;

* It is, alas, lost. But it was certainly written.

condemns landowners and their parasitic royalties on coal and raw materials; touches on the Irish question, bimetallism, education, housing, transport (which he considered should be subsidised to enable urban workers to live in the country), and on trade unionism, which he praised as just and valuable, even if employers could not always see issues in the same way. But at bottom he thought the interests of employers and employees were the same. The manual worker, he urged, needed books and music to refresh him after his day of physical labour – indeed he needed them more than the office worker, who would be better refreshed by sport and the country-side. 'We want,' he concluded,

> 'to take human nature as it is, but to give it a better chance. We want the people to know more of the secret beauties of the glen, of the glories of the moor, of the spacious beauties of the upland; and, beyond everything else we hope to see them drink deeper at that greatest of all fountains of refined pleasure, literature.'

By that time he had been ten years in the firm, to which he had been recalled from school at the age of seventeen. At almost the same age he lost his mother. For the next four years he worked on the factory floor wearing, to use his own words, 'the linen jacket of a soap boiler'. On coming of age he was called from the stench and physical labour of the vats to become a partner, and one of his first steps was to extract £2,000 from the firm to construct a new building in which the hitherto wasted by-product glycerine could be treated and sold. His uncle George sneered about wasted money, but glycerine was very soon to be one of the firm's most important sources of prosperity. Arthur's romantic temperament did not exclude either a practical knowledge of chemistry or a perception of business opportunity.

But it was not in production that the new partner was destined to work. Perhaps it was Arthur's imaginative talent that influenced his father in assigning him to sales, or perhaps it was the insolent arrival of an upstart wholesale grocer from Bolton, William Lever, who started making soap next door to Crosfields, and selling it, not as 'soap' but as 'Sunlight'. Later in life Arthur became a friend of Lever's, but now it was his job to fight him, which he did with considerable energy and imagination.

Until Arthur took over, Crosfields had spent little on advertising, but now the budget soared. He got a prominent article about the firm (it bears all the signs of his enthusiastic style) into *The Illustrated London News*; entered the Liverpool Exhibition of 1886 with a stand in the form of an Indian temple entirely made out of soap; and launched a shower of competitions with soap prizes (under Crosfields' new brand name 'Perfection') distributed from the backs of a flock of llamas Arthur bought at a circus. At the same time he was in charge of the whole distribution system, with seventy-three agents under his control at home and throughout the world.

Though they were unable to stop Lever's expansion, the firm went from strength to strength, not only in soap but in other products with an alkaline base. In this they were much helped by their association with Brunner, and his highly qualified German partner, Mond, who had established themselves in the sodium flats of Cheshire to produce alkalis, and notably soda ash, Crosfields' principal raw material. Arthur Crosfield's father John helped Brunner and Mond during their earlier struggles, and a symbiosis between the two firms developed, part of which was a preferential price to Crosfields for soda ash, against all other buyers. German chemists for Crosfields' new laboratories were poached from Brunner and Mond, and Arthur's father in due course became chairman of their firm, which would in the end become Imperial Chemicals. Thus the stage was set for the deadly battle between Brunner and Mond on the one hand and Lever on the other for control of Crosfields which developed early in the next century and eventually left Arthur in search of another role.

Arthur was always very close to his father and eagerly supported John's second marriage, which was as defiant as his first and offended the family's adopted Anglicanism as much as the earlier one had alienated the Friends. John Crosfield's choice was his deceased wife's sister, and Arthur urged his father not to hesitate, 'no matter what a bunch of bigoted bishops might think'.

He inherited his father's keen Cobdenite liberalism, with its hostility to the privileged world and its belief in the 'industrious classes' of which both working capitalists and the proletariat formed a part. From the time of Arthur's grandfather the family had directed and financed the Liberal cause in Warrington. They founded a rival to the Tory local paper and twice won the seat from the Greenall representative of the Tory brewing family who regularly appeared to represent the town. John Crosfield was a personal friend of Bright, and declared he would 'follow Mr Gladstone through thick and thin'.

Towards the end of his life John Crosfield began to travel abroad, and often took his son with him. They went to the South of France and as far as Pompeii, where they pondered together over the ruins of a Roman soapworks. They ventured even further, to India and the Far East, and Arthur began to catch the charm and complexity of Empire, and in particular its contrasts of scenery, about which he later wrote *A Pilgrimage of Empire* in one hundred and thirty-nine correct and well-polished Spenserian stanzas.

By this time – we are now in 1896 – John decided to turn the partnership into a limited company, though he was still careful to restrict the shareholding to members of his immediate family, excepting only the brilliant industrial chemist, K E Markel, whom he had poached from Mond. Arthur was made Vice-Chairman, and on the death of his father in 1901 became Chairman of the third largest soap manufacturers in the world, and (in our values) a millionaire. He was thirty-six.

One other thing needs to be said about Arthur's industrial career up to this time, and it proved to be very important. He became concerned in industrial diplomacy, first within his own industry, and then as

Honorary Secretary of the Allied Trades Association of the Northern and Midland Counties, a forum of employers where, as *The Times* put it in his obituary, he showed himself 'an able commercial diplomat, capable of dealing with industrial disputes and crises'. The same tribute can be found in the brief response of the soapworks' Trade Union leader to Arthur's speech at the works gala in 1892. There is no record of a strike at Crosfields during the many years Arthur was associated with it, but the workers' spokesman did glance at past differences, resolved, he said, by Arthur's 'fairness to those who worked under him, and his desire to see them happy in their individual positions'. Often, in clashes between his fellow-employers, Arthur would urge what he called 'his old Quaker maxim': 'if you are making a decent profit, let the other fellow live'.

This experience, and the many friends it brought Arthur in the industrial north proved to be a decisive factor in the campaign for the Kenwood Estate as public land.

His chairmanship of the company, which began in 1901, saw unprecedented expansion and diversification as a result of investment in applied research. Bank Quay began to make Persil – first of detergents – caustic soda, margarine, even paint and cement. Total sales more than doubled between 1899 and 1911. The workforce shared in the firm's prosperity in the form of better conditions. Hours were dramatically reduced without loss of wages; paid holidays came in; medical and dental care was offered free; premiums were given for attendance at evening classes, which were made compulsory for younger employees; long service was rewarded by gratuities; and health and safety precautions were ruthlessly enforced, with instant dismissal as a sanction for their breach, for in the minds of the management welfare and discipline were interrelated. The holiday concession, for instance, had to be gained in each case by good time-keeping. Perhaps the most remarkable innovation was the unilateral introduction, with the support of the workforce, of daylight saving, a cause Arthur had particularly at heart long before it became law. As he told a derisive House of Commons in 1909, speaking in support of one of the earliest daylight saving bills (it was thrown out), it gave the workman more time for outdoor recreation and kept him out of the dismal, unhealthy pub, his only consolation in the hours of darkness.

After his triumph over the brewing Tory Greenall in 1906 brought him into Parliament, Arthur soon began to look for a wider world in which to find scope for his talents. He took interest in national politics, and travelled more to the South of France, where he was a member of the Cannes Club, one of the smartest on the Riviera, and notable for its golf course.

Its President, with whom Arthur became a close friend, was the exiled Grand Duke Michael of Russia, who will also play a part in the Kenwood story. The two shared a passion for golf, for which the gigantic Romanov – he stood more than six foot six – had to use specially lengthened clubs. He was an exiled cousin of the reigning Tsar Nicholas, but had been required to give up his rights of succession and live abroad on account of his marriage.* Arthur soon became the club's golf Captain, and in 1905 went in for, and to the delight of his friend, won the first national open championship ever held in France.

Now, a national golf champion, an MP, and Chairman of a highly successful company in which he held more shares than anyone else, he fell in love and married. He was about forty when he met Domini Elliadi, who was some twenty years younger. Their first encounter, so family tradition runs, was on the tennis court. He was good at tennis, but she was better. She had already won several tournaments, and quite soon would be able to compete with the greatest women players of her time. Domini was a Greek Smyrniot, but her father, a prosperous business man, had become British and lived at Stockport, not far from the Crosfields' family home.

Tennis was not Domini's only accomplishment. She was dramatically beautiful, highly intelligent, and could match great virtuosos as a pianist. In fact she was a winner, and with this character had boundless social ambition, to which her husband was no more than incidental. He had much heart, she very little. His family did not approve of her, so this

---

* It is difficult to see why. His bride was the beautiful and accomplished Countess Torby, a direct descendant of Pushkin. She was not allowed to be described as a Grand Duchess, and her husband had to obtain a title for her as a favour from the Grand Duke of Luxembourg.

last of the defiant Crosfield marriages took place in Paris with triple ceremonies blessed successively by an Archimandrite, an Anglican Bishop, and the British Consul-General. Domini wore one of the most brilliant Edwardian wasp-waisted wedding dresses.

That was in 1907, a year, also, when a promising political future seemed to be opening before Arthur Crosfield. In May 1907, still a back-bencher of not much more than a year's standing, he entertained the Prime Minister (Sir Henry Campbell-Bannerman) and 'several members of the Government' at the Hyde Park Hotel, and the sequel quickly followed. On 27 June he made his maiden, but far from non-controversial, speech in the House of Commons on an issue which was soon to convulse the political world – the future of the House of Lords. This was very much an opening shot in that great battle. After praising the Prime Minister, and referring to the Party's programme of reform, Crosfield went on:

It amounts simply to this, that after due pre-cautions against hasty legislation, yet without undue and dangerous delay, the will of the people should prevail. I am afraid it must be said not only that the House of Lords has resisted many measures urgently needed by the people, but that when racial passion ran high (he was referring to the riots over Chinese cheap labour) they had not used their undoubted influence to allay it. I believe in full responsibility being laid on the elected chamber . . . I am thankful that the Government mean business on this question.

His most notable friend among the Liberal chiefs was Lloyd George, with whom he was on close terms for many years, and there can be no doubt that in accordance with his family tradition he contributed generously to Liberal funds. There is a well-vouched story that when playing golf with Lloyd George and Sir Alfred Mond at the height of the Suffragette agitation the game was interrupted by what seemed to be two young men who rushed towards the golfers shrieking, 'Give women the vote, you wicked men!' Lloyd George was so rattled that he brandished his club and roared, 'Go away, we're trying to play golf,' whereupon the interrupters revealed themselves as Domini and Mond's wife Violet.

Soon after Arthur's marriage – and partly because of it – an irreparable rift set in between him and his two brothers, Joseph John and George, and led to the eventual loss of control by the family over the business founded by their grandfather. As in many Victorian and even Edwardian businesses majority shareholding lay with members of the family, but even in the last days of their father the three controlling brothers had not got on. Arthur as the eldest had most shares, but the other two were in a combined position to outvote him, and the three frequently disagreed about large and small management questions. Arthur's enthusiasm for the welfare of the workforce made his brothers uneasy, and so did his sensitive attachment to principle. He opposed

a proposal by Joseph John to shave a minute
quantity off the weight of a leading brand and sell it
in the same package with the same price, arguing
instead that if the costs of production had risen, they
should charge another halfpenny for the same weight
as before. Above all, the brothers differed about
their relations with the two predators who now
threatened them: Lever, whose qualities of dynamism
Arthur admired, and Brunner/Mond, whom his
brothers preferred. Arthur disliked Brunner, and his
brothers detested Lever. Personal preferences went a
great way in those days on questions which might
now be the subject of impartial analysis. Arthur's
disappearance from Bank Quay's day-to-day work
in favour of the world of politics, society and sport,
and his ill-advised marriage added to, but did not
create, the discord between him and his brothers.

In 1909 the two younger brothers combined to
oust Arthur from his chairmanship, and in 1911
from his place on the board as well, and an arrangement with Brunner and Mond gave Crosfields a few
more years of precarious semi-independence. But in
1913 Brunner and Mond came to terms with Lever in
an understanding from which the respective scopes
of Uniliver and ICI still flow, and two years later
Crosfields finally fell to Lever.*

* This agreement, which might be called 'The Treaty of the Acid
and the Alkali', was made at Lever's extraordinary house 'The
Hill' at Hampstead. Following the defeat of Brunner and Mond
in their attempt to patent a process of hydrogenation which
would have made them undisputed monopolists in the manufacture of margarine, they surrendered all their soap and fat

Arthur Crosfield

As a result of this struggle between the two great predators Arthur Crosfield, the largest shareholder in the prize for which they contended, became a very rich man. He needed to be, for he was now committed to allowing Domini to build the largest private house in London. With its sixty-four rooms it was designed round her talents by the architect Hubbard – a vast ballroom, a music room capable of holding four grand pianos and a large audience. A full length portrait of Domini by the fashionable de Laszlo presided over the gorgeous furnishings. In the seventeen acres of grounds were four tennis courts – two grass, two hard – and the only evidence of Arthur's presence was his modest collection of water-colour landscapes by George Sheffield, a little-known northern contemporary whose work had attracted him. Arthur, with his romantic and liberal outlook, wanted to call the place 'Witanhurst', the name by which it is now known, but Domini, for some reason, always preferred '41 West Hill'. Her reason was certainly not modesty, but may have been his frequently expressed inclination to leave it ultimately for some public purpose. In the meantime, perhaps, he was not sorry, remembering his Liverpool palace of soap, to compete with Lever,

interests to Lever, who agreed in return to leave them undisputed possession of their alkali interests provided he benefited by the special price for soda ash they had traditionally given to Crosfields. Lever had much the better of the settlement, and Crosfields as an independent firm was doomed. The agreement in the long term set the boundaries for expansion of Uniliver and ICI.

whose pergolas at 'The Hill' were spreading at the other end of Hampstead ridge like the tentacles of his acquisitive personality.

It was not an accident that just before 'Witanhurst' began to rise Arthur's old friend the Grand Duke Michael reappeared on the scene. He paid Arthur and Domini what was almost a state visit at Warrington, while Arthur was still its MP. Royalty was a rarity in Warrington, especially in such impressive form as the giant Grand Duke and his beautiful wife, accompanied by a spectacular retinue. There had been a civic reception, a procession, a guard of honour from the local regiment, speeches and interviews well reported in the local press, and a well-publicised tour of the Bank Quay soap works. There was also a great deal of golf playing by Arthur and his guest at Hoylake.

The sequel was the Grand Duke's tenancy of Kenwood House, negotiations for which began not long after his visit to Warrington. There is every reason why this should have been encouraged by the Crosfields. It adjoined 'Witanhurst'. Domini adored him, particularly because he was in a position to unlock many doors in the highest society. Arthur liked and admired him. Most important of all, having Kenwood occupied by so distinguished a tenant for a reasonably long period ahead would frustrate any schemes the Earl of Mansfield might be meditating for developing the slopes bordering 'Witanhurst'. Arthur was far too experienced a business man not to have picked up such rumours.

So, in 1910, the Grand Duke moved into Kenwood

House, with all its Adam furnishings and family pictures, under a twenty-one-year lease at £5,500 a year.* This included the whole estate, on which Michael promptly laid out a golf course, which can be seen on the Kenwood Preservation Council's map stretching westwards from the present Highgate women's bathing pond along the fringe of the South Wood. It was an easy stroll for both the old friends for an undisturbed game.

In the first of the tumultuous elections of 1910 Arthur hung onto his seat at Warrington by a slender one hundred and fifty-four votes; but in the second he was defeated, and his parliamentary career was never resumed. The second parliament of 1910 was prolonged until 1919, by which time his ambitions in that direction had evaporated – though not, it should be added, his contacts in the higher reaches of the political world. Asquith, Balfour, and in particular Lloyd George, remained correspondents and visitors.

In June 1914 the lights shone once more on the terrace of Kenwood for the Grand Duke's house-warming ball. Eight hundred guests, among whom Arthur and Domini must certainly have been, were presided over by King George V himself, accompanied by Queen Mary. All must have seemed to those present as it still had been.

But it was not. Almost in the same week as the Grand Duke's ball *The Times* Estates Correspondent reported that 'inquiries point to the fact that there

---

* See the Kenwood Rent Rolls in the Mansfield archives. Lord Mansfield was entitled to bring the lease to an end in 1920, but not earlier, and this he did.

has been a renewal of offers, similar to those which have been made on previous occasions, to acquire Lord Mansfield's estate in Hampstead for development'. He also pointed out that there could be difficulties in view of the existing tenancy, and that the land was of 'great importance in relation to Hampstead Heath'.

What followed is a matter for the next chapter. The purpose of this one is to show that from the very beginning of the struggle over Kenwood, when at times the question seemed to be totally submerged by world events, there was a man of wealth, influence, business experience and idealism living on the borders of 'The Northern Heights' and free to make rescuing them his cause. In fact, Arthur Crosfield was at that time searching for a cause to absorb his restless energy, and provide him with a world in which he could escape the overwhelming personality of Domini. He loved Kenwood, as one can see in all he wrote about it, he knew it well, and it was in his interest to save it: and above all the principle of saving it for the public corresponded to one of his leading ideals.

The First Shots

Rumours of the Earl of Mansfield's intentions had begun to circulate as early as 1908, and among other ears they reached were those of the public-spirited Earl of Meath, a former member of the LCC and current chairman of the Metropolitan Gardens Association, who took a step of decisive importance. In December 1908 he approached the Earl of Mansfield and extracted from him an undertaking – imprudent on the Earl of Mansfield's part – that if he decided to sell the estate he would in the first place offer it to a public body, preferably the Metropolitan Gardens Association. This pledge may have influenced the Earl of Mansfield to defer such a difficult decision by accepting the Grand Duke as a tenant shortly afterwards, for after all the value of the property could only grow during the twenty-one years tenancy he granted, and Lord Mansfield was only forty-four. Moreover the lease allowed a break after ten years. In the meantime a substantial rent from a wealthy tenant would be valuable in itself and relieve the Mansfield Estate of a large bill for maintenance.

It is difficult, however, to see why, after his agreement with the Grand Duke and his undertaking to Lord Meath, Lord Mansfield appears to have decided to sell in 1914. Apart from incurring Romanov indignation, he overlooked the fact that Kenwood was a highly newsworthy property: and he could hardly have let it to a more newsworthy tenant. In 1913 an article had appeared in *Country Life* entitled 'Ken Wood: the Home of HRH the Grand Duke Michael of Russia' with copious illustrations.* The piece was a curtain-raiser to the great ball entertaining King George V that followed a few months later.

The announcement of the proposed sale in *The Times* (whose Estates Correspondent was to be a campaigner for the rescue of Kenwood throughout the struggle) was careful to point out that there should be no hurry, for the Grand Duke would surely remain undisturbed; but it set the alarm bells ringing. Worse followed. A map was published in 'a certain newspaper' showing a closely packed network of terrace housing and streets as the objective of the developers who, it was said, had approached Lord Mansfield. A meeting was hastily convened at which the veteran Heath campaigner Lord Eversley presided, and Lord Mansfield's agent was present. So was Lord Meath, and the pledge of an offer to the public was revealed. The reply on behalf of Lord

---

* *Country Life xxxiv* 710: These illustrations have great historical value, since they give us the last evidence of the Adam furnishings and other ornaments in their precise arrangement dating back to the time of the first Earl of Mansfield.

Mansfield was that when the time came such an offer would be made, and that the price was £550,000.

This mountainous price – something like £22 million of our money – had a great effect on all that subsequently happened, and was generally denounced. It was £2,500 an acre, far more than building land in London usually commanded. £550,000 was a quarter of a per cent of the entire outgoings of the Exchequer in that year – enough to make any Treasury official blench. Many saw it as no more than an attempt by Lord Mansfield to evade an awkward undertaking. And then there was the question of the sitting tenant. One could hardly throw out or buy out a Grand Duke, so a private developer would have his money locked up for several years to come.

Despite all these drawbacks the meeting resolved on an attempt to devise a purchase scheme, and adjourned. That decision was swept away in the rush to war precipitated by the murders at Sarajevo a few weeks later. But the question of Kenwood's future was not wholly lost. Much went on during the war years, for there were several anxious watchers who were not willing to let the matter drop.

The Grand Duke continued for some time to reign at Kenwood. He became chairman of the local hospital, graced public occasions, and when the Zeppelins began to fly, and anti-aircraft guns appeared in his grounds, he was glad to entertain the officers and tell them about his own campaigns long ago in the Caucasus. In 1916 he gave another splendid reception. This time to celebrate the

1 *Above: The March of the Guards to Finchley* by Hogarth

2 *Left:* William Murray, first Earl of Mansfield, aged 74

3 *Above:* The Bank
Quay Soapworks in
1886

4 *Right:* Arthur
Crosfield, aged 41

5 *Opposite:* The
Mansfield Estate from
'Witanhurst', early
1920

6 *Above:* Wedding of
Venizelos at
'Witanhurst', 1921
(Venizelos and his
bride [to his right] are
in front. Domini
Crosfield is on the left
[with camera], with
her husband Arthur
to her left and slightly
behind. The lady on
the pillar is Domini's
sister, married to a
Greek admiral, who is
on her right.)

7 *Right:* Lloyd George
and Venizelos at
'Witanhurst' in the
early 1920's

8 *Opposite:* The Heath
Mosaic – acquisitions
and cost 1879–1979

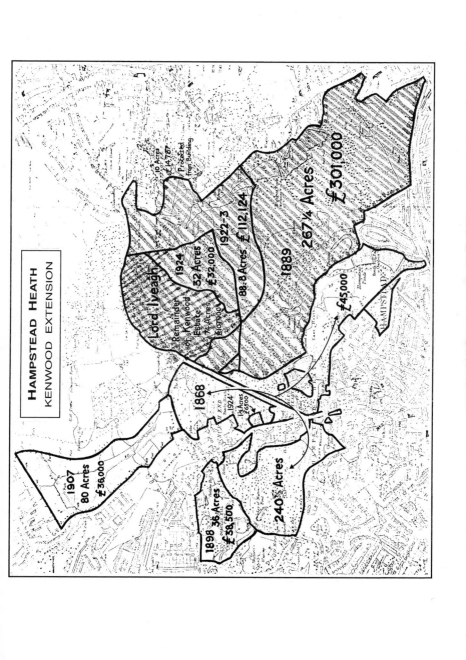

HAMPSTEAD HEATH
KENWOOD EXTENSION

Lord Iveagh

1924
52 Acres
£32,000

Remainder
of Kenwood
Estate
74 Acres
£107,900

1922-3
88.8 Acres £112,124

1889
267¼ Acres
£301,000

£45,000

1868

1924
1½ Acres
£5500

1907
80 Acres
£36,000

1898
36 Acres
£38,500

24.0½ Acres

SAVE KEN WOOD,

Hampstead Heath & the Northern Heights for London.

9 *Above:* The First Appeal (1920)
The photographer, almost certainly Crosfield himself, must
have been stationed on the edge of the South Wood, near the
south-east corner of the lily pond. The prominent conifer on the
far bank bisects the view of the house, to show the Orangery on
the left and Lord Mansfield's library wing on the right.
The North Wood rises beyond the house.

10 *Above:* The First Earl of Iveagh

11 *Below:* King George V inaugurates the new public lands of Kenwood, 18 July 1925

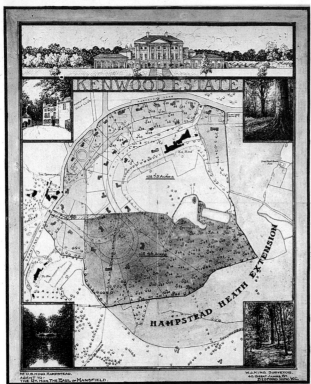

12 *Above:* Plan to develop villas, drawn for C B King and W J King, c1923

marriage of his younger daughter, Nadejda, to no less a person than George V's cousin, heir to the marquessate of Milford Haven and brother to the future Earl Mountbatten. Nadejda's elder sister Zia was not to be so lucky. Only a year later, when she married Harold Wernher, son of the fabulously wealthy diamond magnate Sir Leo, the Russian revolution had deposed the Romanovs and sharply reduced the Grand Duke's means.

'Witanhurst', in the meantime, had been turned into a hospital, and Crosfield, in 1915, was raised to a baronetcy. The honour was sudden and unexplained, since Arthur was not to any appearances engaged in war work, which is surprising in view of his keen patriotism and long business experience. True, he and his family had always been loyal Liberal supporters, and had contributed generously to party funds, so a natural explanation would be that the honour was the not unusual counterpart of such help, even though Lloyd George was not yet Prime Minister or leader of the party.

But although Liberal donations no doubt played a part in Arthur's baronetcy, a further and more interesting reason may be suspected, and since it throws light both on the man and indirectly on the history of Kenwood, it should be mentioned. Arthur was at that time developing a close friendship with that stormy petrel of Greek politics, Eleutherios Venizelos, who was at that time Prime Minister of Greece. The introduction, no doubt, had come through Domini but the two men had taken to each other and such a connection would have been of great interest to the British Government. The question of whether a still neutral Greece would enter the War was being fiercely contested between the pro-German King Constantine, and his pro-allied Prime Minister Venizelos. In the end it was to cost King Constantine his throne, and Greece joined the allies.

Whenever Crosfield was in Greece, as he often was, he had no hesitation in showing his public sympathy with the Venizelist cause. He saw Venizelos as a true friend of Britain and a true liberal, and when Venizelos visited England, whether he was in or out of office, he usually included a stay in 'Witanhurst'. When, in 1921, he married for a second time, his bride was already a close friend of Arthur and Domini, and the wedding breakfast was held at 'Witanhurst'. Later, after an assassination attempt in which Venizelos' wife was seriously wounded, the couple stayed there to recuperate. Even as late as 1934 we find the Crosfields accompanying Venizelos (now again Prime Minister) to Crete for a tour of Sir Arthur Evans's latest discoveries at Knossos.

Arthur's romantic imagination was stirred by Greece and its scenery, just as his admiration was caught by the fire and courage of its great politician. Later on his Hellenic enthusiasm was to cost him dear, but there can be no doubt that at this time the British Foreign Office would have valued his influence and popularity. He and Domini both received Greek decorations, and were granted the special privilege of wearing them in England, as an exception to Queen Elizabeth I's rule (still observed) that 'my dogs shall wear no collars but mine'. It is not difficult to see Arthur's baronetcy as in a measure a compliment to his powerful friend and a gesture to good Anglo-Greek relations at a critical moment of British war policy.

Venizelos, however, even if his visits gave lustre to 'Witanhurst', could hardly be a direct ally in the cause of Kenwood. For that we must look to Lawrence Wensley Chubb, who deserves more recognition today than he has received, for he was the first man to make what we call 'the environment' his professional career. To his campaigns we owe the earliest controls on outside advertising, smoke abatement and the furtherance of many other such causes, particularly access to the countryside, recreational opportunity, and the rescue of open space. He founded the Ramblers' Association, rescued Box Hill and the Surrey Commons, and became the greatest authority of his time on rights of way, footpaths and public open space.

This remarkable man was originally an Australian of modest family, who came to London for his education and completed it at the Borough Polytechnic. While there he developed an enthusiasm for country walking, and in 1895 began to speak on the subject in the debating society whenever he could. As a result he caught the eye of Octavia Hill, who used to attend the debates as a member of the public, and was then meditating one of her favourite projects, the National Trust. By her influence he became Secretary of the Kent branch of the Commons Preservation Society, whose chief was Lord Eversley, and soon afterwards Octavia Hill made him the launching Secretary of the National Trust. But after a short time in that post he returned to the Commons Preservation Society, now as National Secretary, and it became the base for his subsequent campaigns.

Chubb must have come into Crosfield's orbit through Lord Eversley, who was also a veteran of many Heath campaigns and had convened the emergency meeting of 1914 on the news that Kenwood might be sold.*

Chubb and Crosfield made an ideal partnership, with Crosfield supplying the business experience, the advertiser's imagination, and the passion; and Chubb the perseverance, the well-grounded advice and, in his Society, an administrative machine.

But Crosfield appears to have fired the first shot in his Kenwood campaign entirely on his own initiative, in a form that was typical of him. In 1916 he wrote to Lord Balfour, Foreign Secretary in the new Asquith

---

* Eversley's long life – he lived to be ninety-seven – was primarily devoted to the rescue of open spaces, though he also had a distinguished political career, sitting in several cabinets under Gladstone and Rosebery. He was concerned in every campaign for the Heath, from its inception in the 1870's through all its major additions (Golders Hill, Parliament Hill, the Heath Extension) up to and including Kenwood, which he survived to see rescued. He was also a leader in the rescues of Wimbledon Common and Epping Forest, and for many years President of the Heath and Old Hampstead Society, in whose archives there are many letters from him. Looking back on his career he said the effort he had devoted to open spaces was the most important contribution he had made in his long life on earth. If anyone deserves a memorial on the Heath, he does.

Coalition Government, suggesting that Kenwood should be bought by the public as a memorial to those who had fallen in the War. Balfour's reply conveyed the impression that this imaginative proposal had been carefully considered, and went on to reflect that war memorials would perhaps be best considered when the War was over.

One would have expected this overture to have troubled the Grand Duke but it does not seem to have done so. Arthur cheerfully refers to it in his final report of the Kenwood Preservation Council, of which the Grand Duke remained throughout a prominent supporter. But any obstacle presented by his tenancy was soon removed by the Bolshevik Revolution after which ('Maximalist Sedition in Petrograd' was the headline in *The Times*) he retired to the more modest surroundings of a flat in Cambridge Gate, Regents Park, leaving the graves of his favourite dogs and, for a time, his golf course as reminders of his presence at Kenwood. He remained the formal tenant, but passed a sub-tenancy to the widow of an American tin millionaire, Mrs Leeds, whose son later married the Grand Duke's niece. But even Mrs Leeds had to go in 1920 when the Earl of Mansfield was able to recall the lease. The way thus became clear for the Earl to resume his plans.

Crosfield and his ally Chubb were quick to appreciate the new situation, and they did not wait for Mrs Leeds in her turn to disappear. They approached the Earl of Mansfield entirely on their own initiative a month before the end of the War – October 1918. Although they had no formal backing,

and no organisation, this date marks the beginning
of the real struggle for Kenwood that was to last for
nearly six years.

They asked for 'an option over a reasonable
period' in which to raise a thousand pounds an acre –
£220,000 – by public subscription, for the whole
property. It was refused, with a reference to the
pre-war asking price of more than double that
amount – £550,000. The offer was edged up a little, to
£250,000, and that too was refused. There the
bidding stopped, and the negotiation ceased.

The fact that Crosfield would venture no further
on his own is a tribute to his business instincts about
what the estate was worth and the level of price that
could be publicly defended. He was testing the water,
and after a long and bitter struggle Kenwood was not
to fetch much more than his final offer of 1919. In the
course of it mistakes were to be made by both sides,
but the most serious distorting factor was Lord
Mansfield's resolution to get the highest possible
price by reference to the initial, unrealistic figure of
over half a million. As the *The Times* was later to
point out, purchase by philanthropists deserves
some concessions by wealthy sellers.

When the discussions of 1918 ended the Earl let it
be known that he would still consider offers on the
basis of a public appeal, so in the early months of
1919 Crosfield set to work creating the engine that
became the Kenwood Preservation Council. From
the very first his campaign was based on two
principles both of which came from Kenwood's
importance to the existing Heath. Since it dominated

the lower slopes – and this applied especially to the South Wood that bounded the upward view – its loss to builders would ruin what had been achieved in previous Heath campaigns. Its acquisition would not be so much an extension as a necessary safeguard for what had been captured for the public so far. It followed that the purchase of Kenwood, if made, would be presented to the London County Council as the authority for the Heath.

But on 10 July 1919 Lord Mansfield announced that the estate was now on the market for the original price of £550,000. This was a declaration of war. And yet it was a war fought at very long range.

Crosfield and Lord Mansfield never seem to have met face to face or even to have corresponded directly with each other. Crosfield himself certainly fired off a great deal of public ammunition, though he carefully avoided all personalities, leaving what he thought to be inferred; but the Earl never said anything and, apart from one short visit to Kenwood in 1920, he maintained a dignified silence carrying out his accustomed punctilious round in his Perthshire properties, shooting, fishing, scrupulously answering letters, and making odd, quirky little notes in his diaries of things that had struck him. Was Zeruiah a man or a woman? Three hat tricks in one cricket match. Quotations from 'Ruthless Rhymes for Heartless Homes' – clearly one of his bedside books.

Occasionally Mr C B King, the Earl's Hampstead agent, would travel up from Church Row to Scone, to take his principal's instructions, or perhaps seek approval of his actions or advice, for he seems to have had considerable discretion, and all business with the Preservation Council was carried out through him. His namesake W J King – perhaps his brother – was an architect whose name appears on the numerous and varied layouts for developing Kenwood which are still preserved at Scone, and resemble a series of battle maps on which the villas, like the units of a defeated army, retire and regroup in ever-diminishing numbers towards the summit of the ridge.*

Crosfield, who considered he was still in negotiation with Lord Mansfield, and had only suspended it to find what support he could get, regarded this as a breach of business behaviour, and *The Times* Estates Correspondent quickly reflected this indignation. The opening price, said *The Times* on 17 July, was 'preposterous' and though 'perhaps as good as any to start from, it is the final figure that will matter if the estate is the subject of serious negotiation'. 'Such estates', it warned gravely, 'move slowly' and it was important to discourage speculators in grounds which were among the most beautiful in London and dominated Hampstead Heath. Lord Mansfield should show public spirit. In a final thrust the writer demanded that the official valuation for rating purposes should be published. These themes constantly recurred in *The Times* campaign, to which Crosfield and Chubb clearly had regular access.

* The line to the 'building syndicate' so often mentioned by the campaigners, but never identified, must have run through the Kings.

Even before *The Times* had delivered its broadside Crosfield had arranged to raise the matter in Parliament in a question to the Prime Minister. It was in the name of Commander Curzon (Winston Churchill's nephew and later Earl Howe, and a member of the Kenwood Preservation Council) but its reference to saving 'the ancient woodlands' bears all the signs of a text provided by Crosfield. It was answered for the Prime Minister by Mr Bonar Law who loftily ignored the suggestion that the Government should help with a purchase and denied having any information except what he had seen in the newspapers.

The suggestion for Exchequer help is not surprising even for that period. The original Heath, and all subsequent major additions to it, had received substantial help from public funds. But Kenwood was to be an exception. If it was to be rescued it would be by private individuals, with perhaps some help from charities and the notoriously penny-pinching local authorities.

This was the background to the formation of the Kenwood Preservation Council at a meeting held in Middlesex Guildhall in the autumn of 1919. The mountainous price sought by Lord Mansfield, and the absence of any sign of public funds, made it from the first a bold, even Quixotic enterprise. Even the London County Council, the authority for Hampstead Heath, when they were discreetly approached through the architect, Sir Aston Webb, then President of the Royal Academy, had been discouraging. The most they would agree to was to authorise their Chief

Valuer, Frank Hunt, and the head of their Parks Department, to attend the Council's meetings as observers. Any direct contribution was ruled out, and no pledge was given that the LCC would even accept the estate if offered as a gift.

Nevertheless, and in spite of these discouragements, The Kenwood Preservation Council was formally launched on what was to be five years of perilous life.

In due course the Preservation Council grew and developed till it began to resemble an elaborate, many-tiered wedding-cake with its vice-presidents, councillors, chairmen and vice-chairmen, but at this stage, in the autumn of 1919, one can clearly see the core that animated it, and provided the leadership. Crosfield was Chairman of the small Executive Committee. Sir Robert Waley-Cohen, who had spent almost his whole career in Shell, and lived at Caen Wood Towers, was a Vice-Chairman, and Henry Goodison a distinguished stockbroker who lived at Fitzroy Park was Treasurer. Both were neighbours of Crosfield and their properties abutted directly on the Mansfield Estate – something that was to be very important later.* Goodison's memorial fountain, designed by the Liverpool sculptor Tyson Smith, and put up after the campaign was over, just between the eastern edge of the South Wood and the Highgate Ponds, is the sole monument of the Kenwood Council's struggle.

* Both were, in fact, tenants of Lord Mansfield for part of their land.

To these three one must add Crosfield's earliest associate, Lawrence Chubb whose organisation, the Commons Preservation Society, with an office in Victoria Street, provided the Council's clerical support and address.

A great deal had to be done before any appeal could be made to the public. Above all a firm figure had to be negotiated with Lord Mansfield, and it had to be less than the only sum he had named so far, which had been generally denounced as outrageous. At the same time impressive sponsors should be assembled, who might not only subscribe themselves, but as declared vice-presidents and councillors would encourage others to subscribe. On top of all this the difficult question of Hampstead and Highgate, the two proud communities at either end of 'The Northern Heights', had to be addressed. The Crosfield initiative was clearly based on Highgate, but another movement to save Kenwood had been launched in Hampstead by Miss Beatrice Osmond, whose father had been secretary of the committee that campaigned to save Parliament Hill and its Fields back in 1889. She had induced a formidable Yorkshireman who lived in Bishop's Avenue, Sir Herbert Nield KC, to put himself at the head of a committee to save Kenwood.

The Highgate-Hampstead diplomacy no doubt took some time but it ended by Sir Herbert agreeing to serve under Arthur Crosfield as a second Vice-Chairman, and Beatrice Osmond becoming Honorary Secretary of the Council. She emerged more than four years later covered with tributes.

Sir Herbert was also a valuable acquisition. He was emotional, yet blunt. He could not believe, he sometimes told his audiences, that the glories of Kenwood and the need for them to be in public hands, could be ignored. He was also an MP and a great power in local government, and in 1923 – in the midst of the Kenwood Campaign – achieved the eminent position of Chairman of the Conservative Party.

Then it was necessary to recruit a president for the splendid array of important people who were to fill the front rank of the appeal. One was found in the Earl of Plymouth. He was yet another of the surprising number of peers who had shown an effective interest in such questions as urban planning and open space, and he had served in more than one Conservative government, his last post having been Commissioner of Works under Balfour. As such he had conceived the great processional route from Trafalgar Square to Buckingham Palace which commemorates British imperial achievement; and after leaving office he had organised the rescue of the derelict Crystal Palace and planted it on the crest of Norwood Hill as a popular amusement resort for South Londoners. His interest in Hampstead had perhaps been stimulated by writing a book on Constable, and he was keen on all sports, especially golf. This popular and active man died in 1923 when his last compaign was on the verge of success.

But the negotiations with the Earl of Mansfield about the price were the main anxiety of 1919–1920. They were, in Crosfield's words, 'difficult and protracted'. They started where Crosfield and Chubb had left them, at £250,000, and produced the only recorded conference of the Earl with Mr C B King (March 1920).

The Council's negotiators were at a disadvantage, because prices were rising rapidly in a post-war boom. Although *The Times* Estates Correspondent did his best to pour cold water on the value of Kenwood, the Earl's agent studied the markets. The Earl refused an offer of £300,000, and then of £320,000 as figures for purchase at an option of one year without deposit. So matters stood in the spring of 1920. Even the Council's negotiators were perhaps influenced in making these better offers by the buoyancy of the market. Should they offer yet more? £350,000 perhaps?

Arthur Crosfield was growing anxious. Time was passing and no general appeal had yet been made, though the proclaimed intention for one was now eight months old. When that moment came he would have a great deal of work to do. But in the meantime he was committed to a semi-public tour of Greece with Venizelos, now again Prime Minister and deep in the post-war negotiations which, in the Treaty of Sèvres, brought Greece for a moment within sight of all its national aspirations and promised a long period of liberal, pro-British government in that country. Venizelos himself had been in London early in April, planning the visit.

These pressures had an influence on the disastrous decision that was now made about Kenwood. Arthur and Domini left Highgate in mid-April with the next offer still unsettled. Their first stop was Cannes, where Arthur had the tricky job of extricating himself from the golf captaincy and installing 'the very capable and most popular' Earl of Wemyss as his successor. This achieved, he was preparing to complete his journey to Greece by yacht when he was recalled to Highgate 'by urgent business'. He turned round and left Domini to sail alone. The business undoubtedly was to close with the Earl of Mansfield on a new firm offer of £340,000. He may have improved slightly on the details in a final struggle, but £340,000 was the least the other side would accept. The option was to run for eleven months from October next. It could be represented publicly as a handsome concession by Lord Mansfield on his original half million, but in his heart Crosfield must have known it was too much.

He set off once more to tour sites which till then had been visited by few British travellers, climbed Mounts Parnassus and Pantelicon, and was in time to applaud his friend the Prime Minister on his triumphant return to Athens on 4 May when he spoke to a crowd of a hundred thousand from the balcony of the Hotel d'Angleterre in Omonia Square. He and Domini were constantly in the company of Venizelos, and Arthur himself spoke at a lunch given in honour of his friend by the Anglo-Hellenic League, scouting British hesitations about supporting a man who had shown himself a true democrat, a European statesman, and a friend of Britain.

Early in June, as a final gesture, the Crosfield yacht took some eighty guests, including the Prime

Minister, on a cruise to Sunium, where the moon-
beams on the temple were enhanced with red and
blue electric lights, and, with a band on board, 'M.
Venizelos unbent the bow'. The Greek papers
thought it had been like 'a bit out of the Arabian
Nights', and as Arthur told the *Warrington Examiner*
in a long interview soon afterwards 'everything went
off all right'.

But he can hardly have been so confident about
Kenwood. There was an appeal yet to be written, an
advertising campaign organised, private approaches
would have to be made to possible donors, and it was
already July. In not much more than a year he had to
raise £340,000 or face failure. It might well not be
achievable and his original judgment had been
against going so far. And now the City columns were
beginning to say – and no doubt his business friends
whispered more gravely – that market values were on
the turn downwards. Even rich men were going to
find themselves a bit short. But he was pledged now,
not only to his colleagues but to himself, and he was
going to see it through. One way or another he was
going to get Kenwood and add it to the Heath.

The Frontal Attack

'SAVE KENWOOD: HAMPSTEAD HEATH AND THE NORTHERN HEIGHTS FOR LONDON' came out in the late summer of 1920. Brief and pungent, in Arthur's typical copywriting style, it bravely sets out the Kenwood Preservation Council's purposes and the reasons for them.

On the front page of the simple fold-over sheet is a picture which has been taken a thousand times since but must then have been new to most of those who saw it. This one was probably shot by Crosfield himself (he was a keen amateur photographer) from a point between the two ponds, and shows the house beyond Adam's intervening sheet of water, distant, almost as if on an island, its startling whiteness emphasised by the dark North Wood beyond. The skill of the photographer creates a frame of shrubs and sedge in the foreground. It is as if the walker, after climbing the hill below and passing through the South Wood, has paused in astonishment at what he suddenly saw.

The picture is in itself a statement that the appeal

was for purchase of the whole of Lord Mansfield's property, whether wild open space, ornamental land, or the house itself; and the aim is clearly repeated in the text that follows with its reference to 'the wonderful tract of unspoilt beauty, containing 220 acres of Park-like land, interspersed with sequestered lakes set amid a screen of rare trees and great banks of rhododendrons . . . flower beds and rose-gardens and stately avenues, an "Adams" (sic) mansion of world-wide fame, and above all, stretches of "primeval" woodland'.

The shot chosen also illustrated what underlay the whole Crosfield approach and was in tacit contrast with the traditional policy on Kenwood established by the first Earl. What that great man and his successors had so valued was the view downwards from the terrace and the library windows towards the distant capital. The front door was on the other side of the house. Crosfield evoked the view upwards from what was now the public land of Hampstead Heath, and the evergrowing capital. The Earl of Mansfield acquired Parliament Hill to preserve the view from Kenwood to the south: Crosfield needed Kenwood to preserve the view from the Heath to the north.

This is why the appeal stresses, in fact exaggerates, the exclusiveness of the estate. It speaks of 'high walls and gates which closely guard the property', and while it is true those exist on the Hampstead Lane frontage, the separation from the Heath was no more than a hedge. Just the same the appeal's case for more access by townspeople to open space in general was effectively deployed. It was Crosfield's favourite theme. He used statistics about the dense populations of Islington and St Pancras, whose lack of recreational space was 'a pathetic example of the lack of foresight of earlier generations'. Epping Forest and Wimbledon Common, large though they were, lay far off to the east and south, and anyway – anticipating a usage then rare but now commonplace – 'no one would suggest that a single acre of these priceless lungs could be spared'. And Hampstead Heath at its present size was smaller than either.

The rather doubtful history that Arthur foisted on the estate was not included in this first appeal, but he was eloquent about the trees, animals, birds and plants which had found refuge in Kenwood and justified describing it 'as a reserve of wild life'. Although he clearly envisaged more football pitches and the like than modern Heath-lovers would approve, his concern for conservation was genuine, and when the Council eventually captured the South Wood it was at their insistence that the wooden fences were installed, which control the walkers and remain characteristic of the place.

The one serious gap in the presentation is the future of the house. There can be little doubt that Crosfield loved it as part of the scenery, but he shows little interest in it or its wonderful furnishings, in their own right. And after all the Council's bid did not even include the furniture. They certainly regarded the South Wood and the Ponds as their ambition, and the house and the land beyond it were included in their bid, but the absence at this stage even of suggestions for possible use of the house is puzzling, for the problem must have occurred to them.

So far as the money was concerned, there seems to have been a tacit understanding with the Earl that he deserved credit for having lowered his original huge asking price, and after all some of that credit could be said to belong to the Council for arguing him into it. The appeal thus passes lightly over the fact that £340,000 – a figure revealed for the first time – was still very high indeed. It was indeed hinted (perhaps as an inducement to the possible subscribers) that Lord Mansfield could get more from the development syndicate with which he was in touch, so he was making a sacrifice if the option was taken up. There is no evidence for assessing this claim, but Lord Mansfield certainly remained in touch with his developers almost to the end.

On one point, however, the Council's appeal did not spare the Earl. It unhesitatingly declared that if they failed there would be 'close development' at Kenwood, and clearly the Council had good reasons for thinking so. Sir Herbert Nield, the most austere of men, referred in a speech more than a year later to having seen a map published in the alarm of 1914 that showed 'the erection of a small type of houses, this meaning innumerable roads'. One can hardly fail to accept what could have been so easily disproved, so the appearance two or three years later of a less alarming development plan showing about a score of genteel villas was clearly a change of approach by Lord Mansfield and his advisers. It was circumstances that had changed. In 1920 and 1921 the Kenwood Preservation Council was fighting complete urbanisation of the whole northern slope from the Spaniards to Millfield Lane, the destruction of the house and both woods and the wild-life to produce a profitable housing estate. By 1923 half the land at stake had been conquered for the public and space was restricted.

The rescuing ranks mustered in the appeal document could hardly have glittered more brilliantly. Thirteen peers (in due course there were to be double that) included a duke, a marquess and a former Prime Minister (Balfour). There were five MPs. Other notabilities included Cecil Harmsworth of the *Daily Mail*, J L Garvin of the *Observer*, J A Spender of the Liberal *Westminster Gazette* and St Loe Strachey of the Conservative *Spectator*. Numerous societies displayed their banners – the Royal Society, the Charity Organisation Society, the Royal Society for the Protection of Birds, the National Trust for the Prevention of Tuberculosis. The Grand Duke Michael was there of course – a Vice-President – and so was another of Arthur's Cannes friends, the Duc de Châtellherault. The Greek connection supplied the sinister millionaire, Sir Basil Zaharov, and the stage the leading comedienne of her time, Irene Vanbrugh. And then there were mayors, but these were uneasily conscious of pressure on the rates. Indeed by that time everyone was beginning to be conscious of financial pressure. But surely such an array would triumph? Some of them could have bought the Kenwood Estate single-handed. Yet as time was to show, very few of them appear on the final list as giving more than a few pounds at best. Their armour shone, but their swords were blunt; and they had been slow in arriving. By that time something like a quarter of the Earl's time-limit had gone by.

The appeal was also supported by a poster campaign on the Underground, which had recently been extended to Golders Green. Its Chairman, the remarkable Lord Ashfield, whose social conscience long left an impression on his railway, may have been influenced also by the traffic which the new open space would attract to his newly extended line. Perhaps, too, he was a golfing partner of Crosfield's, for golf was his favourite game. At any rate the posters came gratis and were the work of the well-known cartoonist 'Poy'.* One shows a pathetic little picnicking clerk, complete with bowler hat, protesting vainly against an axe-whirling ruffian labelled 'Jerry Builder' who is in the act of felling a tree under which the napkin has been spread; another a desperate hare hunted by a brutal builder with two dogs labelled 'bricks' and 'mortar'. Kenwood continued for long afterwards as a favourite subject for some of the finest posters the Underground produced.

Despite all this effort the money trickled in slowly and in small amounts as the eleven months of the option ticked away to the deadline of 1 September 1921. The depression was deepening, and purses were closing. There was a coal strike. Although the

* Percy Fearon.

Hampstead and Highgate Expess kept up its fire, *The Times* – so loyal hitherto – fell singularly silent. It was clear that £340,000 was not going to be raised by half-crowns and guineas. Surely some of the great men advertised on the first page of the appeal could come forward with large sums to encourage the public?

Whatever was going on behind the scenes during the winter of 1920-21, there was very little outward demonstration of activity by the Council. There was no rousing fund-raising event, or monthly publication of subscription lists. The last flutter of interest in the national press had been a discussion stimulated by the Egyptologist, Flinders Petrie, who lived in Cannon Row and suggested Kenwood might become the headquarters building then being sought for London University. There was very little to be said for the idea except perhaps Petrie's own convenience, and nobody could accept his assertion that 'the few ancillary buildings' and sports facilities he envisaged would not in fact ruin the landscape. There was also his alarming idea for a tram-line along Hampstead Lane and the Spaniards, which, after descending the hill would link Kenwood with Petrie's other work-place in University College, Gower Street. He joined the Kenwood Council, where his vision seems to have been effectively muffled, for no more was heard of it.

There was an external factor that winter which diverted Crosfield's attention – or at any rate his opportunities for public campaigning. Again it con-cerned Venizelos, whom we last saw in triumph with

Crosfield at his side in June 1920. In the following month the Greek armies drove the Turks back across Thrace almost to the gates of Constantinople, and in August the Treaty of Sèvres gave Thrace, most of the formerly Turkish Aegean Islands, Gallipoli, and in effect even Smyrna, to Greece. Two days after signing this glorious (but never-fulfilled) document Venizelos was leaving Paris for a return to Greece when he was shot and wounded by two Greek royalists at the Gare de Lyon, and a virtual civil war broke out in Greece between his followers and the royalists. Things were further complicated by the death of King Alexander (whom Venizelos had substituted for his enemy King Constantine) from a bite by a pet monkey.

The outcome of these extraordinary events, which Arthur and Domini had followed with fascination and horror, was the return of King Constantine and the defeat of Venizelos in a turbulent general election. In November 1920 the man who had led Greece to the brink of fulfilling all her ambitions was driven into exile, leaving his country to the mismanagement of the royalists and the disastrous defeat of the Greek armies by the Turks in Asia Minor.

Venizelos had never been well off and, although he remained, even in exile, a major political figure both in his own country and in Europe, he was now almost penniless, and entirely dependent on sympathisers in the West, among whom the Crosfields were prominent. Through them he had met a Miss Helena Schilizzi as along ago as 1913. She was one of Domini's dearest friends, and was also rich. He was a widower, and sought the company of Helena Schillizzi almost as soon as he was driven from Greece; and in 1921 they were married, with the reception at 'Witanhurst'. His extraordinary career was not yet over, and Helena was soon nearly killed at his side in yet another assassination attempt. In short, there were many pressures on Arthur Crosfield at this stage of Kenwood's history, and his support of the Venizelist cause went well beyond hospitality and speech-making. It went deep into his pocket. What with the cost of 'Witanhurst', Domini, and the Greek liberals the recession must have seemed even more serious to him than to those he was beseeching on behalf of 'The Northern Heights'.

In the spring of 1921 the organisers of the appeal, alarmed by the feeble flow of donations, at last decided on a more vigorous programme, of which the first sign was an article signed 'Londoner' in, of all places, The *News of the World*. The author was simply described as 'a distinguished correspondent' and may well have been Crosfield himself, for he faithfully reproduces Crosfield's arguments and style. Twelve days later the Preservation Council (by kind permission of the Earl of Mansfield) held a reception at Kenwood for sympathisers. The man from *The Times* added pathos to his report of the occasion with comments on the neglected appearance of the shrubbery, and the dustsheets in which the pictures and furniture were now muffled as in a house soon to be abandoned. 'Miss Shotter's pupils performed some beautiful dances'. Crosfield and Nield made speeches. Time, they stressed, was running out. Crosfield clearly foresaw the criticisms that would be made when the option expired and the money was not available.

All this was reinforced by a second appeal document which had been prepared by *Country Life* (but the text is pure Crosfield with its 'feathered songsters' and rather unreliable historical associations).* The language is far stronger than before. The acquisition of Kenwood was 'for the benefit of London as the greatest ornament of the capital and the Empire'. Kenwood's value as an open space would be ever-increasing 'as the great civic tide, which has long swept round and past the neighbourhood, develops into another vast area of population to the north'.

But in other parts of the second appeal one detects a new, and more cautious note. This commander, though still cheering on the cavalry charge he is leading, is already thinking about what he will do if it fails. Though in an interview he gave to the *Observer* (25 June) Crosfield bravely denied the Council were over-optimistic, and pointed to the strength of their case, the document issued in June hints at lesser

* He may have been right about 'the last noble remnant of the ancient Forest of Middlesex', and even (at that time) badgers, kingfishers, and green snakes. But the 'duelling ground' in the South Wood and Boadicea's last battle-field (which he placed somewhere near the present Goodison Fountain) are fictions, and the idea of Pope pacing the Lime Avenue is an historical impossibility. His friend Lord Mansfield did not buy Kenwood until ten years after the poet was dead – as a writer in the *Hampstead and Highgate Express* was quick to point out.

objectives. The calamity of building, he wrote, 'can only be averted if men and women of wealth are found willing, with wonted generosity, to provide the sum needed'. Clearly he was now thinking in terms of large donations as the only way out, and he significantly speaks in terms of payment by instalments being acceptable. Then he goes on:

> 'Outlying parts of the estate might, as a last resource, be sold subject to stringent building conditions designed to preserve the amenity of the neighbourhood. Nevertheless, even then, a sum of at least £250,000 must be forthcoming if the central and essential portion of Kenwood is to be saved.'

These words are the germ of the ultimately successful strategy of advancing piece by piece. It is likely that this was the point when Crosfield turned away from the hope of extracting large sums from the grandees of the Council and small donations from the public in general, and began approaches to men he had known in his days as Chairman of Joseph Crosfield and Sons and, before that, as Honorary Secretary of the Allied Trades Association of the Northern and Midland Counties. Men who had grown rich in cotton, ship-building and concrete, as well as soap.

Zealous efforts were also made to stir local authorities to action. Nield and Crosfield made personal representations to several neighbouring councils with some apparent success in spite of the agonising level of rates which, as the *Hampstead and Highgate Express* noted, had gone up from 9s 8d in the pound in 1919 to 14s 6d in 1921. Nevertheless quite large sums – £20,000 or even £30,000 – were spoken of by some councils and even made the subject of resolutions. But here there was a technical difficulty which it would take time to overcome, if it could be overcome at all. It was considered to be beyond the powers of metropolitan boroughs to subscribe directly to a private charitable appeal such as the Kenwood Preservation Council, especially if its object lay outside their boundaries. The only way round this restriction would be to channel municipal contributions through the London County Council as the ultimate recipient of Kenwood, and this needed a policy decision by the LCC which had certainly not yet been taken.

So all that Crosfield could do was to 'bank' the goodwill of the local authorities against the day when private money would have bought enough of Kenwood to convince the LCC that a serious proposition was on offer.

The calendar moved inexorably towards the end of the option period set by the Earl of Mansfield: 1 September. The coffers of the Council held nothing like the required purchase money. The glittering squadron was riding to a fall.

Defeat Turns to Victory

The option died a painful death. Lord Mansfield refused a renewal of any length unless the Council put down £34,000 – ten per cent of the purchase price – as a non-returnable deposit, and in addition undertook to maintain the land in question until they paid the rest. Apart from the hardness of the conditions and the folly of accepting them, the Council did not have cash available even for the deposit. They begged for a month, and when that ran out, for another three weeks, which were both granted, so the option remained convulsively alive for nearly another two months.

The Council put up a frantic struggle. The fund-raising events at Kenwood became weekly occasions. Queen Mary herself was induced to take a walk on the Heath after an official visit to open the nursing home near the Whitestone Pond which until recently bore her name, and asked no doubt suitable-looking passers-by what they thought about saving Kenwood for the public. Crosfield and his colleagues deputed yet more earnestly to various local authorities, and

Crosfield himself addressed a meeting of London
MPs which elicited a resolution of warm support –
but nothing more. A special reception was held for
'public men and the press' at Kenwood, after which
the *Hampstead and Highgate Express* became speech-
less with enthusiasm:

> No spoken or written word can portray adequ-
> ately (it exclaimed) the sublime effect of the
> wonderful stillness and unspoiled beauty of
> those 200 acres.

But *The Times* knew a sinking cause when it saw
one, and only two days after the option expired it
published a leader which was in effect an obituary. In
tepid discouraging words it reflected that perhaps
there was no great urgency about buying Kenwood
after all, and it might be a luxury which in these hard
times should be deferred; thus dismissing the fact
that Lord Mansfield's developers were only waiting
for the word go. A prompt rebuke was published
from Sir Sidney Colvin, the Keats scholar, who had
just headed a successful appeal to save the Keats
House and was a friend of Crosfield's, denouncing
such desertion of a cause the paper had so loudly
supported. But there were other eminent fainthearts.
Lord Eversley, triumphant in so many great Heath
campaigns and a member of the Council, wrote in his
own Society's organ *Commons Forests and Footpaths*
that, although Kenwood was '*almost* (my emphasis)
indispensable to the enjoyment of Hampsted Heath',
the LCC had not agreed to accept it, and the times

were unpropitious for additonal public expenditure.

The Council now began to be widely criticised for having grandly embarked on a foolhardy adventure. The Estates Correspondent of *The Times* returned to his earlier theme that the price had been too high in the first place, and an independent valuation should have been obtained before an appeal was launched. From this it was an easy (though unspoken) step to hint that a wealthy proprietor was entitled to ask what he liked, and a committee of wealthy proprietors seemed happy to acquiesce and ask the public to open their purses accordingly. But had *they* put their hands into *their* large pockets? They had been long about propaganda and organisation, but short on progress reports.

These points were made in a powerful letter to the *Hampstead and Highgate Express* by the prolific popular novelist George Bergin, who said he would be happy to subscribe if he knew how the price had been arrived at and who had subscribed so far. The Council should be more open. This stung Crosfield into a correspondence with two letters (19 November and 17 December) in which he revealed a great deal about both the campaign and the direction of his own thoughts. In the first of these he disclosed that the resources currently available to the Council amounted to the pathetic sum of £53,000 including (uncashable) local authority promises of about £40,000. The subscriptions from individuals had been a mere drop in the ocean of the price demanded by Lord Mansfield but, he went on, 'within a month we hope to have a guaranteed amount of more than £100,000 – indeed nearer £150,000'.

By this time many readers would have thought this was mere whistling in the dark. The second defiant letter was in reply to cries that the price the Council had agreed to was too high. He abandoned all pretences that it had reflected any generosity on the part of Lord Mansfield, and recited the stages of hard business bargaining through which it had been struck. It was simply the least Lord Mansfield would accept, and if people thought it was high they were right. 'May I say at once that that is, and has been, the opinion of those who have been striving to save this estate.' But the demand for an independent valuation was beside the point, because Lord Mansfield was under no obligation to sell at all, and could ask what he liked. He would not accept anything which would prejudice his negotiating position, and requesting it would merely have broken off any prospect of a deal. He ended his letter of 17 December with this:

If, towards the expiration [of the option] our Kenwood Preservation Council had arranged for an independent valuation, in the hope of getting the price substantially reduced, they would have taken the most effectual steps to destroy any prospect of the renewal of the option . . . We have proceeded with our work with the firm conviction that if public-spirited boroughs and . . . public-spirited individuals assist us in raising large sums . . . Lord

85

Mansfield would in all probability assist us to complete the work by himself making a large contribution.

From all this it is plain that Crosfield was in no mood to give up the struggle and had reached certain conclusions about how to carry it on. The attempt to buy the whole estate at a stroke could not go on, and it would be necessary to proceed by stages. The new sources of donation he so optimistically talked about, large though they were, could not reach to anything like £340,000. The local authorities had shown, in his contacts with them, that they would only be willing to give if victory was assured, and at a reasonable price. Large private donations were essential if there was to be any prospect of municipal money.

The source of these donations, about which Crosfield had spoken so confidently, could only have been tapped by Crosfield himself. None of his colleagues had his industrial background, and it was to the world he knew best – the world of Midland and Northern industry – that he turned. He cashed his reputation as a large and a popular employer, and his conspicuous part, as Honorary Secretary, in the Northern and Midland Allied Trades Association, which had earned so much goodwill of a lasting, northern kind. Between mid-November 1921 and January 1922 the immediately available cash (ie not counting local authority promises of future help) rose from a figure which must certainly have been less than £20,000 to £86,160 11s 5d. By the summer of 1922 it had surged to £132,000.

We do not know how widely Crosfield's northern canvass had stretched, but the decisive donations, though only three in number, came to £90,000. Only with these could the campaign have recovered.

Mr William Whittingham of Harrogate gave no less than £50,000 – a cool million in our money – making him one of the greatest benefactors the Heath has ever had. He appears to have been connected with ship-building. The other two really large donors, F C Minoprio of Liverpool and T W Wilkinson of Carnforth contributed £20,000 each. The Minoprios were descended from an Italian immigrant to Liverpool who had made a fortune. It is not quite clear whether the donor was the grandson or the great-grandson of the original Aloisio Vincenzo Minoprio, because both had the same initials, but the older man seems the more likely candidate.* Thomas William Wilkinson had inherited the huge fortune built up as a pioneer of reinforced concrete and cement by William Boulton Wilkinson, and was the author of two books on roads, *Highways and By-Ways of England, their History and Romance* and twenty years later, *From Track to By-Pass.*** next page

* The name of Minoprio did not become nationally celebrated until 1934, when Miss Gloria Minoprio appeared at the Ladies' Open Golf Tournament wearing trousers, and completed her round using only one club. She did not win, but her costume elicited a public protest from the Ladies' Golf Union. She long continued to adorn the championship.

There were several other sizable donations during the autumn of 1921 and the spring of 1922. A Mr Muir MacKean of Paisley contributed £4,000, the City Parochial Charities £3,000 and the Poulter Trust £2,500. The recently ennobled Lord Glendyne, Robert Nivison, who lived at Branch Hill Lodge and was a close adviser of Lord Leverhulme, gave a handsome £3,050 – the largest of all the private Hampstead donations. Crosfield himself subscribed £1,250 in his own name, which looks rather modest until one remembers it is the equivalent of £50,000 today. He was no longer so rich as he had been – the building of 'Witanhurst', Domini's other extravagances, and his support for the Venizelist cause had eaten into his fortune. An exception which appears only on the last of the subscription lists the Council published was for £25,000. It was anonymous, but annotated, 'introduced by Sir A Crosfield'. Some of it could actually have been his own money, or was collected by him from close personal friends. One suspects it conceals some local names – perhaps that of Lord Leverhulme, with whom Crosfield had been on close terms of friendship for many years, as letters of Crosfield's in the early 'twenties show. Another could have been the richest of all the Hampstead

---

** When Joseph Crosfield and Sons diversified in the 1890's one of their important new products was high-quality cement. H W Wilkinson's two books contain many interesting anecdotes and pieces of information, but are primarily calls for better and more efficiently planned roads; and frequently mention reinforced concrete.

millionaires, Lord Iveagh, but of this there is no evidence.

Naturally this dramatic increase in funds correspondingly increased Crosfield's influence in the campaign. He appears to have been in the chair of all the remaining meetings of the full Council as well as Chairman of the Executive Committee, and when in 1923 the President, Lord Plymouth, died, he was not replaced. Another sign of Crosfield's pre-eminence was much fuller information about the progress of the campaign, including the names of the main subscribers. But it was still made clear that, though perhaps more slowly, the intention was still to acquire the whole estate, and especially the South Wood.

In January 1922 the full Council met and took stock of an improved, but still difficult situation. Their report, issued immediately afterwards (21 January), recited the whole course of the campaign so far, and revealed the change of tactics during the slump which had bedevilled the campaign. Finding the possible major donors, with whom they had meant to start, had proved unresponsive, they had been driven to a general appeal and pressure on local authorities. The Council now accepted that the original chance of buying the estate as one, was dead, but there was now enough money to embark on a scheme of partial purchase. The Council seems to have put up something of a struggle against the Executive Committee having full control of the next stage, and its determination to give up discussions with Lord Mansfield about buying the whole estate.

He would not abate his price, said Crosfield, and a letter asking him if he had employed an independent valuer in reaching it had been ignored. On that issue, which was in effect acceptance of the policy of partial purchase, Crosfield used the words 'The Committee would be willing to continue' and in effect asked for a vote of confidence.

At this point I have to bring in, and dispose of, a question which aroused much suspicion and mystery during these months, and indeed earlier. The Kenwood Council's official utterances had always emphasised the necessity of advancing to the north, but several of its leading supporters including Crosfield himself had houses and large gardens abutting the Highgate boundary of the Mansfield land. Just what schemes were discussed, and when, is not fully on record, but at one time an idea seems to have been current that as much as fifty-six acres on the Millfield Lane side of the Heath should be sacrificed to developers who would be induced to enter into strict amenity covenants in return for a price below what the Council paid to Lord Mansfield. This was argued, no doubt, by saying that a subsidy from the Council to create a leafy suburb round Millfield Lane was a legitimate use of Council funds and would leave the Council free to concentrate on the Northern Heights. The scheme got out, and caused whispers that were unfavourable to the Council. It survived only in a much smaller and quite harmless form, which was to be directly helpful to the capture of the South Wood without sacrificing any Mansfield land to development.

In the spring of 1922 Crosfield made full use of his discretion to reach agreement about just what offer to make to Lord Mansfield for a partial purchase. The great advantage of the policy was, of course, that the price could be matched to the particular parcel chosen, and this was ninety-five acres of open land, much of it sloping and marshy, some of it ponds, and all difficult to develop profitably. It seems that in parting with it Lord Mansfield would sacrifice only ten villas. Crosfield offered £135,000 – £1,444 an acre, or nearly £200 an acre less than had been agreed for the whole estate. It included the land between the existing LCC boundary and the eastern edge of the South Wood and then northwards as far as Hampstead Lane to take in the Highgate Ponds and everything as far as Lord Mansfield's eastern boundary. They tried to get the South Wood, or at least a bit of it, but Lord Mansfield insisted that this was not on offer. 'It was worth too much as building land.' So the deal was concluded on 22 July 1922, with completion in six months time. Fortunately the Council was now working within its means. Crosfield signed the contract without further formal reference to the Council, which did not meet to approve the transaction until October.

One wonders how many of the prestigious names were attending by this time. Those of them who were present on 22 October at Middlesex Guildhall were told that the purchase to which they were already committed would come to nearly £140,000 including expenses, chiefly stamp duty, towards which there was already £132,000. As a precautionary measure they were advised to authorise the selling on of nine acres of the proposed purchase to three 'riparian owners' in Highgate to raise just over £12,000 in case there was a shortfall. In the event it was not needed for this round, but came in very useful for the next. All this was to be completed, without further reference to the Council, by Crosfield, Nield and Chubb who were appointed trustees of the land to be bought until it could be handed over to the LCC and 'dedicated as an open space to the people'.

Even these small sub-sale agreements caused suspicion of self-interest by the Council, three of whose leading members were enabled to protect their already handsome properties (and enhance their value) with a belt that could never be developed, though it belonged to them. But they can be defended as benefactors of the purchase scheme, since they paid a development price for land they would not be allowed to develop; and helped the Council's cash flow, if not its total resources. But the decisive argument for the arrangement was that the LCC officials, with whom Crosfield and his allies were in constant touch, made it clear that whatever land the LCC might accept (and it had so far accepted none) it did not want these remote glades near Fitzroy Park, which would be expensive to maintain and patrol. This was advice the Kenwood Council could not reject without the risk of finding the Mansfield land permanently on their hands, even if they managed to buy it. Indeed at one time it almost looked as if this would happen.

The agreement to sell nearly half of the Kenwood

Estate did not mean that Lord Mansfield had
abandoned his intention to develop what was left to
him, though a new scheme on a smaller scale would
now have to be prepared. But during the early
months of 1922 the whole contents of the house –
books, pictures, furniture – were reviewed and
decisions made about what would be removed to
Scone Palace and what would be sold. The auction
was held in the summer. Much of the furniture
specially designed by Adam, which had stood in
chosen positions for a century and a half, was
dispersed. Although the Preservation Council had
never taken much interest in the house and its glories
within, and had preferred to dwell on its scenic
qualities, the auction made a melancholy impression.
It showed Lord Mansfield was serious, and the
empty house continued its reproachful testimony for
the next three years by falling steadily into decay.

Mr C B King, the Earl's agent, was commissioned
to produce a new development plan for the smaller
area, of which one version was printed, probably in
1923.* It shows thirty-three villas linked by a number
of curving access avenues spreading from Hampstead
Lane, and over the North Wood and the West

* A number of variants survive in the Mansfield archives.
Unfortunately they are undated, and it is not clear which, if any,
were approved. The most ambitious shows forty-seven villas,
though oddly enough none appears in the South Wood. On this
plan there is also some development on the Elms Estate,
including a road – 'Kenwood Drive' – starting not far along the
Spaniards' Road from Jack Straws. Some of the plans contain
jottings about the large prices paid for adjoining land.

Meadow. It is not clear what was to happen to the house itself, but the implication is that the North Wood would largely disappear, while the South Wood survived. If so there must have been an earlier, and different plan. The Mansfield Estate's insistence that the South Wood had too high a building value to be sold to the conservationists is otherwise incomprehensible.

Lord Mansfield and his advisers never seem to have penetrated the intentions of the Preservation Council in its new phase. Their publicity had shown again and again that the South Wood was their real objective, and even in the last negotiation they had tried to include it. He allowed them in the agreement of 22 July to get to its very edge. He even surrendered, in negotiation with the cunning Chubb, the right on which he had originally stipulated, to build approach roads and lay drains for his intended development over the open land he was now selling. He was mistaken if he thought Crosfield was going to give up now.

The contract was completed on 19 December, a day or two before the set period expired, and the trustees became owners of nearly one hundred acres which were, from then on, effectively part of Hampstead Heath. They were looked after for the time being by two gardeners based on a shed at the bottom of the grounds at 'Witanhurst'. This strange state of affairs – the only period in which private trustees have been responsible for part of the Heath – lasted the surprisingly long period of eleven months. The confidence of *The Times* was restored, and it prominently displayed a map of the new acquisition under the heading 'Kenwood Preservation: Land Acquired', followed by a long article.

It had been a punishing year for Crosfield. The whole campaign had nearly foundered in humiliation and disgrace. The folly of the Greek monarchists, anticipated by Venizelos, had led to the total defeat of the Greek army in Asia Minor and the sack of Smyrna in which tens of thousands of Greek inhabitants were massacred or driven into exile by the Turks. The Crosfields took a little Smyrniot boy into their family at 'Witanhurst'.

Capture of the South Wood

As soon as the ninety-five-acre purchase was completed, Arthur Crosfield made for his beloved Cannes, whence he launched the next phase of the battle. His letter to *The Times* printed 12 January 1923 shows clearly that he saw himself as at the head of a campaign that was not going to stop short at the fringe of the South Wood:

> Hotel du Parc
> Cannes

> . . . On many occasions when it has been my privilege to address various meetings of borough councils in North London I and my colleagues have been repeatedly assured that, if only men of means would come forward and give a really strong financial lead, the borough councils would instantly and gladly follow it and give the purchase scheme their own powerful financial support.
> Well, handsome reference has already been

made in your columns to the princely generosity with which some of our most public-spirited citizens have given the very lead for which the borough councils stipulated. It is earnestly to be hoped that that lead will now be followed [by purchasing the rest of the Kenwood Estate]. Such a move would, I am sure, have the backing of the London County Council.

He went on to make it plain that he hoped his own Council would buy the whole of what was left, including the house itself, 'so that the public could be admitted to enough of it to benefit by its extra-ordinary beauty'.

This letter must have been read with some anxiety by officials in both County Hall and the town halls. County Hall was by no means converted, at this stage, to the acceptance of paying for the regular maintenance of a large new open space, and although the borough councils had professed enthusiasm and talked about handsome sums, they now began to see that they were going to be under pressure to turn their professions into cash. Lord Mansfield's price would be high. Like the Town Council of Hamelin they felt –

'Besides, our troubles have made us thrifty.
A thousand guilders! Come, take fifty.'

If Lord Mansfield was to be persuaded to sell more, could not something be done to make him accept less per acre for the South Wood?

The trumpet call summoning up the reserves of local authority goodwill had been sounded by Crosfield, but the strategem under which they were to play their part was the work of Alderman Frank Howard, of Hampstead Borough Council, acting in concert with Lawrence Chubb. Fortunately the interval imposed by the complicated negotiations on the sub-sales in Fitzroy Park, which took nearly six months, gave time to work out the stratagem – the wooden horse, as it were – that would carry the purchase campaign into the wood itself.

Alderman Howard was deeply skilled in local government questions. He was soon to be Mayor of Hampstead, and was already one of its most senior politicians, a member of the Kenwood Council's Executive Committee, and Vice-President of the Heath Protection Society. Surveying the Earl's defences he detected drainage as one of their weaknesses. He knew well that the drainage from Kenwood represented a problem. It always had been so, even when it had to cope with only one large house. For a large development a new drain would be indispensable, but where should it run? It could not run uphill to the main sewer along Hampstead Lane and the Spaniards' Road, and it would be inordinately expensive to lay it across the land now belonging to the Kenwood Council all the way to the sewer along Highgate West Hill, though Lord Mansfield had carefully reserved the right to do this, and to build access roads there for the estate he still hoped to build. The only other handy main sewer available ran beside the Vale of Health, but the way to it lay across land which had long been part of the Heath and was owned by London County Council.

C B King, Lord Mansfield's agent, and his architect relation were now working on the layout of an estate of villas for the territory that remained, and embarked on discussions with Chubb and Howard (separately, the evidence suggests, though they were in league) on the subject of the drain; and as a result what looked like a deal emerged. The Mansfield Estate would surrender to the public a narrow strip along Hampstead Lane which was much needed for widening that road; and would abandon its reserved rights to build drains and roads over the Preservation Council's newly acquired land. In return Hampstead Borough Council and the Kenwood Preservation Council would support Lord Mansfield's application to the LCC for permission to carry a drain under the Heath to join the Vale of Health sewer. It is to be feared that the consent Chubb and Howard gave to this – though they kept their word – was not wholly sincere support for an application their experience must have taught them the LCC would turn down, which they duly did. The price of the support – unavailing as it proved to be – was duly exacted in the abandonment of all Lord Mansfield's rights to build drains over Kenwood Council land, and he was now tied firmly to the single possibility of the Vale of Health.

Chubb and Howard then came forward with a fresh deal. If, they suggested, the Mansfield Estate would concede a strip – eight acres perhaps – of the South Wood's fringe for permanent preservation 'as a nature reserve' and in the interests of the upward view from the Heath, the LCC might yet be persuaded to concede the drain under the Heath. They offered no purchase money, because the land concerned would still form part of Lord Mansfield's property. All that was required was a convenant that would preserve at least the illusion that the heights were crowded with woodland. By the late summer of 1923 the thing was done.

The coup was reported in *The Times* of 19 September, with the remark that 'if the scheme was carried out it is likely to facilitate steps for the preservation of the rest of the woodland', and (as the Kenwood Preservation Council said blandly in its final report) the concession 'substantially reduced the building value'. A few days after *The Times* announcement Alderman Howard confided in the Heath Protection Society (the minute is struck through for some reason, but is surely authentic) that after 'protracted negotiations he had got Mr King to recommend that the whole of the Woodland up to the skyline should be handed over to the LCC' in return for access to the Vale of Health sewer and surrender of his rights across the Preservation Council's land.

King did not realise that he had been outmanoeuvred, and redesigned his scheme of development in a brochure which must belong to the latter part of 1923. He saw clearly that none of the villas he hoped for could now be placed on the twenty-four acres of the South Wood (even if cleared) immediately behind the barrier between them and the upward view which

Howard and Chubb had so ingeniously preserved; but he still dotted thirty-three of them along Hampstead Lane and over the West Meadow, connecting them with pleasantly curving avenues, and he even showed 'the line of the proposed drain' with an optimistic dotted line.

But even before the plot had thickened as it did in the autumn of 1923, Crosfield had rallied the local authorities to the breach that was being created. The sub-sales on the Highgate side had been an excuse for inaction, but within a few days of their being completed (28 July) he told *The Times* that –

> another opportunity may shortly present itself for acquiring such additonal area of property, including a splendid remnant of the old Middlesex Forest, in which, it is interesting to note, several families of badgers are still actively at work. Should the Borough Councils specially interested, with the approval and support of the LCC, at any time endeavour to acquire such an additional area of property, a useful nucleus of a further fund will be available in consequence of the sub-sales effected by the Kenwood Preservation Council.

The lodgement on eight acres of the South Wood was also brought to bear on the hitherto prevaricating LCC itself. In October 1923 they received a long and detailed letter from the Kenwood Council setting out the whole negotiation about the land hitherto acquired and asking the LCC to take it over

101

as soon as possible: but that cautious body, having granted authority for the now famous drain, waited to see what would happen to the forces now being assembled for the final assault.

It took a long time to marshal them. In February 1924 Howard could tell the Heath Protection Society no more than 'there was a probability of the whole thing going through' and the Society resolved that if it did the South Wood should be subject to the same rules of opening and closure as Golders Hill Park. At last, in April 1924, stung by the persistent questions of one of its members, a Captain Frazer, the LCC resolved to accept the land the Kenwood Council was so far able to offer.

It was probably this decision, combined with what Crosfield afterwards described as 'the sterilization' of the South Wood so far as building was concerned, that led Mr King to advise Lord Mansfield that it would be best to sell the whole wood for what it would fetch, and embark on a negotiation. Twelve authorities,* apart from the LCC and the Kenwood Council were involved in it.

The price negotiated was a bare £1,000 an acre, £400 an acre less than the Preservation Council had paid for what they had so far bought. It was low

---

* The London and Middlesex County Councils, Finchley Urban District, the Metropolitan Boroughs of Hampstead, Hornsey, St Pancras, Islington, Paddington, Shoreditch, Hackney, Kensington, and Stoke Newington. The remainder of the Kenwood Council's funds also went into the purchase money.

enough to bring in even the poorest London local authorities north of the Thames (such at Shoreditch), and by spreading the load it allowed the richer ones (such as Hampstead) to pay a good deal less than the handsome contributions they had once talked about. Nevertheless the distribution was graduated with the poorest and most distant authorities paying least. In June it was announced that 'sufficient money had now been collected', and early in the autumn of 1924 the deal was completed by which Lord Mansfield sold the thirty-two acres of woodland on which 'so high a building value' had only recently been placed; the property transferred including not only the wood itself but the two ponds and a strip to their north, bringing public access to a direct view of the house.

'PURCHASE SCHEME COMPLETE: ANCIENT WOODLAND PRESERVED'. So *The Times* of 18 November, using the largest print it then allowed itself, reported. There was a page of pictures too, which for *The Times* was a recent and daring innovation, and a leading article: 'News that should rejoice the hearts of all Londoners who value open space'. It began:

A large part of the Kenwood Estate, the property of LORD MANSFIELD, has been purchased for incorporation in Hampstead Heath. The whole acquisition is by no means the whole of that estate, but amounts to 120 acres out of 220,* and comprises all that the public-spirited purchasers have in mind, namely the fine timber and the illusion it is so important to preserve, of

103

unspoilt woodland when viewed from the lower slopes of the Heath . . . Had Kenwood, or those acres of it that have been preserved, gone the way of so many other open spaces, the adjoining part of the Heath would have suffered a curtailment, and a loss of dignity which would have taken away much of their charm. The Heath, thanks to Ken Wood, has always looked much larger than it is . . .

The joy of *The Times* did not end there. In the next issue Crosfield was accorded the singular honour of a 'turnover' or signed article, which was reserved for special occasions. In it he related the whole history of the campaign from its origins to the stratagem devised by Alderman Howard which had 'the effect of sterilizing from building some acres of Kenwood' and led to its purchase. He warned the public there would be some restrictions on the new territory to protect its wild life, and concluded in the well-chosen words:

The addition of Kenwood will crown the achievements of those who have sought to enrich the most diversified, picturesque, and popular of London's pleasure grounds.

---

* Like many acreage figures published at the time, these are not quite accurate, and do not do full justice to the achievement of the Kenwood Council. The total of their two purchases was 130.8 acres of which ten were later sold off under covenants.

The sub-editor on *The Times* who wrote the headline for the Kenwood story asserted that the Kenwood purchase had been 'completed', but outsiders who had followed the matter could still see Lord Mansfield in control of the house and seventy-four acres around it. Perhaps the journalist knew better, but it was enough to cause a dignified letter from the Earl of Meath, who had started the whole question in 1914 by revealing Lord Mansfield's promise to make an offer to the public before selling. In it he rehearsed the whole story of how Lord Mansfield had had to be reminded of that promise, and thereupon 'without demur' had made an offer at the price he was to get from the building syndicate. It was sad that the War had prevented the offer from being pursued at that time, but he would like to bear witness to Lord Mansfield's straightforward dealing and sense of honour in keeping his promise. He even sent Lord Mansfield a copy of the published letter with a short personal letter congratulating him on his 'highly honourable conduct'. Perhaps, under the thirteenth Earl of Meath's courtesies lay a sense that after twenty years, aristocratic honour was now satisfied.

Final Act: Lord Iveagh

Amidst all these rejoicings and self-congratulations one troublesome little phrase in *The Times* leader puzzled those who read it. The new purchase 'comprises all that the public-spirited purchasers have in mind'. It was dexterously inserted, and can only have come from the Kenwood Council itself. Surely, the public began to reflect, Crosfield and his allies were not giving up when they were on the threshold of complete victory? Not long ago they had been singing the praises of the rest of Lord Mansfield's estate and the need to get it too for the public. The North Wood, they had said, was second only to the South Wood in scenic importance. The Lime Avenue, the Rose Gardens, the house itself, with its historic interest, had yet to be saved from the builders. Where was the clarion call for the last push that would drive this menace from the Northern Heights for ever, and complete the greatest open space in London? Several letters to this effect were printed in *The Times*, and many more poured into 'Witanhurst'. In the midst of their glory, Crosfield and his colleagues were deeply embarrassed.

On 5 December Crosfield found it necessary to answer these critics by himself writing to *The Times*. The key passage in his letter was in the following carefully chosen but mysterious words:

> Although I am not at liberty to say any more at the present time, it can now be definitely stated that not a yard of the 76 acres of Ken Wood will ever be sacrificed to builders. It is with the utmost satisfaction, Sir, on unimpeachable authority, that I am able to state this for the information of your correspondents and of countless others deeply concerned about the ultimate destiny of this ancient and historic property.

Whose was the unimpeachable, but undisclosed, authority? Undoubtedly that of Lord Iveagh, who took over the house and its surroundings three weeks after this letter was written. The conclusion must be that at the time the purchase of the South Wood was being completed (as it was on 19 November) Iveagh's interest in the remainder of the estate was known to Crosfield and his associates, and that an understanding of some kind was reached between them and Iveagh. To understand this curious part of the story it is necessary to say something about Lord Iveagh's history and character.

Edward Cecil Guinness, first Earl of Iveagh, is described in his *Times* obituary as 'a quiet man'. So quiet was he that despite his many and generous philanthropic achievements, his colossal wealth, and his considerable political influence, no biography of him has been available to this day, and his entry in the Dictionary of National Biography quotes no source but *The Times* obituary already mentioned.*

The careers of Edward Cecil Guinness and Arthur Crosfield bear some resemblance to each other, though Guinness was much the older, having been born in 1840. Both of them inherited successful manufacturing businesses in which they worked hard on leaving school (sixteen in Guinness's case) and both retired on capitalisation in middle life to devote themselves to politics and philanthropy. But with those features the resemblance utterly ends, for in every other way they were opposed in character, beliefs and achievement; and also in wealth. Guinness turned his brewery into a public company in 1886 (ten years before Arthur Crosfield's father did the same for Crosfield and Sons) in the most spectacular flotation of the century. It raised £18 million (nearly

---

* 'Available' needs explanation. The well-known author George Martelli wrote a life of the first Lord Iveagh (*Man of his Time*: a Life of the First Earl of Iveagh KP, GCVO) in 1933, but copies were and are restricted to the Guinness family. Martelli also wrote a life of the second Earl, his son (*Rupert Guinness*; a Life of the Second Earl of Iveagh KG, CB, CMG, FRS) which was subject to the same restriction as that of his father, as was H S Guinness's *Richard Guinness of Celbridge* (1934), of which only twenty-five copies were printed. There is no published history of Guinness, Mahon & Co. I therefore depend primarily upon Michele Guinness's history of the family, *The Guinness Legend* (London, 1989).

a billion of our money) of which Edward Cecil
Guinness retained one third in Guinness shares. Just
why the shares in a brewery – albeit one of the largest
in the United Kingdom – should have attracted such
support must be left to the explanation of economics,
but it can be safely said that the subsequent history of
the company amply justified the confidence of its
investors.

Only a year before the flotation Edward Cecil
Guinness was raised to a baronetcy 'for services to
Ireland' by Mr Gladstone. The *London Gazette*
reporting this, commented that 'he is anything but an
ostentatious man. Perhaps his failing is that he is
rather the other way – that he is rather retiring – if
not timid. His wealth is boundless'.

So indeed it was, and its boundlessness grew
through the rest of his long life. Three years after the
flotation he retired from active management of the
brewery. He rose, by successive steps, to be a baron,
a viscount, and an earl, and became not only one of
the richest men in Britain, but in the world. His
benefactions were enormous. He devoted huge sums
to housing the poor in both Dublin and London,
built and endowed the Institute of Hygiene, and not
long after his retirement from Guinness began his
intervention in the art market, of which the fruits can
still be seen at Kenwood House today.

The intervention lasted four years, from 1891 to
1894, and was anonymous. His agent was the
celebrated Duveen, whose most valuable clients were
American millionaires competing against each other
for European masterpieces, and against them only

Lord Iveagh (as he now was) had the wealth and inclination to enter the lists. In those four years Duveen, who at that time lived at the Elms as a tenant of Lord Mansfield, assembled two hundred works of the highest quality which otherwise might – almost certainly would – have been shipped across the Atlantic; a celebrated Rembrandt, a magnificent Vermeer (one of the score or so in the world), Gainsboroughs, Reynolds, Romneys. The collection is eclectic, but today almost priceless. It was hung in Iveagh's house in Grosvenor Square.

He had a number of houses, the principal being Elvedon Hall in Suffolk, whose oriental magnificence (installed by the Maharajah from whom he bought it) he not only retained but extended. There he regularly entertained King George V, whose recognised personal adviser on Irish matters he became. Despite his great expenditures and benefactions his wealth grew. At the time of his death in 1927 it was declared at £11 million – roughly half a billion today: and this did not include either the part of the Mansfield Estate he had bought or the pictures destined for it.

It has been said already that despite their common business background Iveagh and Crosfield were profoundly different, and not only in measured wealth. Iveagh was the supreme representative of the 'beerage' which Crosfield and his ancestors regarded as the most baleful interest of their times in terms of politics, society, economics and health. Crosfield was a Liberal, Iveagh a Unionist; Iveagh regarded Irish independence with horror and dismay, but

Crosfield was a home-ruler; Crosfield prided himself on owing his fortune to honest manufacture of a commodity that made for health and decency. In his eyes Iveagh's huge wealth had been made at the expense of idleness, waste, ill-health and crime.

They must nevertheless have met even before Iveagh's interest in Kenwood began to develop. One of his favourite residences was Heath House, near Jack Straw's Castle, overlooking the Heath and on the road to Ken Wood. With whatever reservations, Crosfield would not have missed canvassing so rich an inhabitant of Hampstead for his cause, nor Domini such a distinguished recruit for her guest list. Similarly Lord Iveagh cannot have failed to observe the gradual progress of the preservation campaign northwards and the increasingly problematic position of his neighbour the Earl of Mansfield. Gradually the idea that Kenwood House, so near one of his own favourite homes, might perhaps house his glorious collection and be a memorial to his achievements had begun to form in his mind. It was a question of seizing the right opportunity, and towards this he proceeded, as was his habit, with definite, but unpublicised steps.

His opportunity came when it grew obvious that the sale of the South Wood to the public was imminent: roughly the middle of 1924 when Alderman Howard had remarked that he thought 'it would go through', and the eight acres of the South Wood were saved. At that time, it must be remembered, Lord Mansfield was still hoping to develop the acres round the house and to its north and the last thing

111

Iveagh wanted was to install his pictures in a gallery surrounded by suburban villas. Moreover, he was used to handling such matters himself, and this feeling would be especially strong where a personal gesture to posterity was concerned. He was not the man to subordinate his personal control of the operation to either a voluntary body, such as the Kenwood Council, or to a local authority. He therefore had to act before the Kenwood Preservation Council got the whole estate.

The secretive habits of Lord Iveagh thus make it likely that his first approach to Crosfield on this subject was in the middle of 1924. Until then the Council's success over the South Wood could not have been depended upon. Crosfield's feelings must have been mixed on hearing of Iveagh's idea. The Council was still committed to conquering the whole Mansfield Estate as open space, and now had a fair prospect of delivering its promise. To lose the final glory after such a long and bitter campaign would be a disappointment – worse, a humiliation. Lord Iveagh's interest had come late in the day, when the battle had almost been won without a penny of acknowledged support from Hampstead's wealthiest inhabitant. On the other hand the Kenwood Council had now fired most of its ammuniton and, although it had spoken vaguely of opening the house for the public, the continuing cost of keeping it up would be a problem which the LCC might not be willing to undertake. Finally, though purchase had been the main weapon used by the Kenwood Council, its real purpose was to save the estate from development, and as the sub-sales on the Highgate fringe had shown, it was ready to use a variety of weapons.

As business men of experience, both Iveagh and Crosfield knew well that rival bidders in the same market do well to agree beforehand to prevent prices hardening against both. If Iveagh entered the market before the South Wood was captured by Crosfield – and Crosfield was determined to have the South Wood at least – the bargain price extorted by the drainage concession might be lost. If that happened the Council would either have to find more money or give up altogether; and Lord Iveagh on his side might in the end find himself having to buy more land than he wanted to fulful his main purpose.*

But one can suspect the understanding between Crosfield and Iveagh went rather further than this. On Iveagh's side it would have been convenient that Crosfield's announcement, after capturing the South Wood, should include a statement that the Council contemplated no more purchases. Crosfield could

---

* Among his many benefactions Lord Iveagh had never shown any evidence of special interest in the cause of open space and recreation – even to the extent of contributing to Crosfield's campaign, when he could, if he had chosen to do so, have bought the whole of what Lord Mansfield had offered in 1919 at the opening price without serious inconvenience. As Crosfield had pointed out in one of his appeals, the purchase money came to hardly more than the cost of a few masterpieces. It is interesting that soon after buying the remainder of the Mansfield Estate, Iveagh contributed handsomely to the initial appeal for Crosfield's next project – the National Playing Fields Association.

113

only have accepted this on one condition: Iveagh must undertake, with whatever reservations about the pictures, that Iveagh should protect the Kenwood Council's decision to leave the task it had set itself apparently unfinished, and ward off accusations that it had betrayed its repeated undertakings to the public. In short, he should guarantee the land he was buying should end up with the Heath. In return the Council would gracefully bow out once they had the South Wood, explaining, if challenged, that there was a purchaser who would save what they had still hoped to buy and add to the Heath.

The existence of a deal of this kind helps to explain the otherwise incomprehensible way Iveagh proceeded to gain possession of the last seventy-four acres of the estate. It was complicated and, one would have thought, unnecessarily expensive. He could have bought it outright. Instead, on 31 December 1924, only six weeks after the Council had bought the South Wood, he took out a ten-year lease of the rest from Lord Mansfield, and paid the whole rent – £51,800 – in advance. This gave him the absolute personal control he needed, leaving the freehold with Lord Mansfield. Just over a fortnight later, on 15 January, his eldest son and his solicitor, having been constituted by Iveagh as trustees for the purpose and provided by him with the necessary funds, bought the freehold separately from Lord Mansfield for £107,900. Thus Iveagh's trustees became Iveagh's landlords. Their trust, as set out in the purchase of the freehold should be quoted, since it is the justification for the Kenwood Council's

114

retirement from the field:

> 'To hold the same . . . upon trust as regards the
> Land as an open space for the benefit of the
> public for ever by way of addition to or
> extension of Hampstead Heath (but so that
> nothing herein shall prevent the enclosure of
> any part or parts of the woods for the purpose of
> preserving the flora and fauna thereon);'

and:

> 'As regards the Mansion House for such pur-
> poses for the benefit of the public as may from
> time to time be determined by the Trustees for
> the time being . . .'

The purchase document went on to say that when the
existing lease had expired, or at any earlier time the
trustees saw fit, they should appoint as their
successors in the trust the 'London County Council
or other authority in whom Hampstead Heath or the
management and control thereof is or may be for the
time being be vested'. And what was more,

> 'On such appointment being made the premises
> hereby conveyed shall become, and shall there-
> after be and for ever remain subject to the like
> conditions and be held for the like purposes in
> all respects (but as regards the said Mansion
> House and Buildings for the additional purposes
> . . . as herein provided) as are or may for the time

115

being or from time to time be applicable to
Hampstead Heath . . .'

Thus, from the time he first bought the last
seventy-four acres of the Kenwood estate, Lord
Iveagh drew a clear distinction between the land and
the house, and the purposes for which he destined
them, though both were in the end to be carried out
by the authority controlling Hampstead Heath.

Iveagh's lease and purchase went unreported for
more than two months, during which those who were
in the know could only keep repeating on the
strength of Crosfield's letter that all would be well in
the end. But at last *The Times* was allowed to report,
on 25 March 1925, that 'by the generous action of
Lord Iveagh the public are assured that ultimately
the whole of the Ken Wood property will be handed
over to it'. The writer went on to recall the work of
the Kenwood Preservation Council and Crosfield's
assurance that not a yard would be sacrificed to the
builders. 'The foundation for that assurance is thus
made clear'. Crosfield's influence with *The Times*
was one of his great assets.

The Kenwood Preservation Council had by then
ceased to exist. On 17 December 1924, just a
fortnight before Lord Iveagh took out his lease, they
held a rather muted meeting at which a final report
was presented, thanked one another, and disbanded
themselves. It had been a stony road, they had
collected much criticism in their five-year struggle,
and although they knew their task was complete,
they could not yet say so. But they had acquired

116

two-thirds of the Mansfield Estate at a figure, proportionately, some thirty per cent less than the owner had originally set them. And by their persistence they had beaten the building scheme altogether. The whole Northern Heights were saved.*

On Michaelmas Day 1924 the last agricultural tenancy had expired on the Mansfield Estate, and on 10 December at a congratulatory meeting held in County Hall Crosfield and his colleagues handed over their purchases to the LCC. The gardeners from 'Witanhurst' were relieved of their duties by the mulberry-clad, trilby-hatted, brass-badged keepers of the LCC, and on 15 January 1925, when the last seventy-four acres passed to Lord Iveagh's trustees, the reign of the Murrays at Kenwood came to an end after a hundred and sixty-one years.

* It is notable that Lord Iveagh registered his intention that his purchase should go to the LCC as an addition to the Heath before he had even made it, and the two months delay in the announcement could well be attributed to the need for County Hall formalities. Nevertheless, Iveagh must have had some assurance on acceptance of his plans before venturing to close with Lord Mansfield. This underlines the view put forward that prior consultation with Crosfield and the LCC was involved.

117

Transformation Scenes

On the morning of 18 July 1925 a large marquee made its appearance on the long-disputed edge of the South Wood, facing southwards towards London over the open rolling land recently bought by the Kenwood Council. Far away to the east, across the wooded declivity containing Highgate Ponds, the mass of 'Witanhurst' was clearly visible. The marquee contained amplifying equipment and a platform on which were ranged rows of gilded chairs.

All through the fine summer morning a crowd was assembling, until there were several thousand of them. They had walked, in fact many of them had marched, across the Heath after taking trains or buses from distant parts of London. Very large numbers of them were children, drawn from many schools throughout North London, marshalled under their teachers. Uniformed youth services, so popular in those days – Boy Scouts, Boys' Brigades, Girl Guides – were there in force, some of them with bands. But the pictures show a large summery crowd of all ages and styles. There was a choir. On the shot showing the western fringe of the crowd one can see a young, recently emancipated woman with her short skirt blowing in the summer breeze, and a few yards behind her an Edwardian lady in her long jacket almost to her knees, and her heavy skirt an inch short of the grass.

In front of the marquee the crowd came almost to the edge of the platform, but to its right hand, or eastern side, towards 'Witanhurst', a large open space was kept by police and boy scouts, and along this, shortly before three, a number of limousines arrived, from the first of which descended the short, bearded, frock-coated King George V and his Queen. Accompanying them were Arthur Crosfield, Domini, and other grandees of the Kenwood Preservation Council. The new land was now to be formally handed over to the public and inaugurated royally as an open space. Also in the party were those who had contributed the lion's share of the cost: Mr Wilkinson of Carnforth, Mr Whittingham of Harrogate, Mr Minoprio of Liverpool, Mr Muir MacKean of Paisley and Lord Glendyne of Branch Hill Lodge. On the platform awaiting them were the twelve mayors and chairmen of London authorities, who were in turn presented to the King and Queen.

Prayers were said by the Bishop of Willesden, and the King then rose to address the crowd in words which show clear evidence of having been provided by Crosfield.

After describing his own pleasure and the Queen's at being there to hand over 'The Park of Kenwood' to the public, he reminded his audience of the earliest

119

stirrings of the movement that had created Hampstead Heath. 'It was the happy conclusion of more than a century's efforts to preserve this line of heights, so that their beauty of forms and vegetation may refresh eyes and minds wearied by continuous streets and houses, and their wide expanse serve as a recreation ground for a crowded city population.' He went on to describe what the movement had achieved. 'The topography of Hampstead Heath and the neighbouring open spaces, dominating as they do London and the north west, makes their preservation of exceptional importance. We [this was an identification with his hearers rather than a royal plural] are deeply indebted to the activity of the Kenwood Preservation Council, to the noble generosity of private benefactors, and to the co-operation of the local authorities and charitable bodies who have contributed.'

The King then launched himself into a yet more lyrical passage, echoing the address Arthur Crosfield had given to his workforce thirty years earlier:

'This fragment of the ancient forest of Middlesex [it was just behind him] retains a wild and unspoilt beauty in vivid contrast to the populous streets below it, and will give town-bred children a glimpse of the magic of primeval woods and meadowland. I am especially glad to hear that the original character of the estate will, as much as possible, be preserved.'

The King was himself an open-air man, and his

favourite residence was among the broad acres of Sandringham. But there was very little in him of the guilt-ridden romantic who put these words into his mouth, and the preservation of wild life had perhaps, for him, a rather different purpose.

He then turned to a passage which probably had its origin in the Parks and Open Spaces Department of County Hall. It contained a majestic warning against litter, and enjoined the need for discipline among the public to whose 'use and enjoyment it was his great pleasure to dedicate this lovely spot for all time'. He was sure 'the foresight and generosity which had secured it would arouse a beneficent spirit of emulation . . .'

The platform party departed, the schools moved off in their crocodiles, and the crowd strolled away, back to their Hampstead or Highgate homes for tea, or down the hill for the railway station or the trams at South End. Not quite all of them. Some stayed on their new possession till late at night, and a day or two later *The Times* printed a sour article 'From a Hampstead Correspondent' who had patrolled the area on the morning after. Broken boughs, empty beer-bottles, and paper bags had greeted him. More keepers, he said, were urgently needed.

The whole occasion was a celebration of the Kenwood Preservation Council's achievement, and neither Lord Mansfield nor Lord Iveagh were referred to. Indeed they are not mentioned as being present. No doubt Lord Mansfield wished to leave the scene with the same silent dignity he had always maintained, but the absence of even a reference to Iveagh

121

is surprising, seeing he was a close personal friend of the King. And he may not in fact have been far away, for he had already taken full possession of Kenwood House, where he had insisted on having quarters carved out for himself so that he could personally supervise the repair of the house and the installation of his collection. Lord Moyne, his grandson, visited him there as a child in the modest two-room flat which was all the builders could quickly create in the crumbling mansion. It is a curious setting for a man of eighty-five and one of the greatest millionaires in the world taking decisions on the future home of his art collection.

Although much verbal fog surrounds the documentation by which Lord Iveagh's intentions were expressed by his lawyers, and finally embodied in an Act of Parliament,* his wishes are perfectly clear from the moment he financed his sons and legal adviser to buy the house and its surrounding acres under trusts he himself dictated. After all that has passed since, those trusts have endured and still endure. One was that the land and indeed the house should pass to the authority responsible for Hampstead Heath; the other that use of the house should be to exhibit his collection to the public, and that if this use ever ceased the collection should revert to his family. These intentions were to be carried out by trustees he had created for the purpose, and would survive. To complete these arrangements an amendment to his will was needed, and this he made on 9

* Those interested in detail should see the Appendix.

December 1926. Less than a year later he died, on 7 October 1927, aged eighty-seven.

The trustees hastened to carry out the first of their main duties only nine months after Iveagh's death. They resolved formally that the house should be used for the picture collection and at a rather muted little ceremony, which by coincidence fell three years to the day after King George V's inauguration of the Northern Heights, the Chairman of the LCC Parks Committee, Lord Haddo, was received by the second Lord Iveagh and the other Kenwood trustees and presented with the freehold of the estate which the first Lord Iveagh had left them in his will. In accepting it on behalf of the LCC Lord Haddo observed that 'this moment crowned the efforts started in 1831 to preserve the high lands adjoining Hampstead Heath'.

This event marks the effective end of private ownership on what had been the Kenwood Estate, and completion of the task which the Kenwood Preservation Council had begun nine years earlier. The extraordinary anomaly that a priceless collection of pictures owned by private trustees hung on walls owned by the public, for ever, on pain of forfeiture if put anywhere else, was among the oddities left to be cured by the Iveagh Bequest (Kenwood) Act less than a year later, which vested the pictures as well in the LCC. But the regime of the trustees over the house and its contents continued until 1949, when their initial endowment of £50,000 had dwindled from inadequacy to absurdity, and rather than see the relapse of the pictures to the Iveagh estate full control passed to the LCC. The trustees disappeared as a separate body. But the trusts did not.

But what of Crosfield, without whom none of this would have happened?

While he was sitting on the platform at Kenwood for that triumphant occasion, his mind cannot have been entirely with what was being celebrated. Only a few days earlier, on 8 July, he had been surrounded by much the same pomp as was assembled now: the crowds of school children, the Boys' Brigades, the scouts and the metropolitan mayors. That had been at the Albert Hall to mark the inauguration of a new venture which corresponded almost exactly with the favourite theme of his life. If not the only originator of what came to be the National Playing Fields Association, he was undoubtedly the most active of them. He had been involved at least from the beginning of 1925, when the idea was developing, and he was Chairman of the Provisional Committee.

The Association's structure bears all the signs of his workmanship, for it reproduces the Kenwood Council's organisation, though on a vaster scale, with its drum-roll of distinguished vice-presidents, its massive 'Council' of well-wishers, and its Executive Committee which included several of Crosfield's circle. Lawrence Chubb had a seat on it, and later became the Association's General Secretary. So did the Canadian sportsman, Domini's close friend, Colonel Mates. Among the founding sub-scribers we find not only Lord Iveagh, but Crosfield's old source of funds, Mr Muir MacKean of Paisley.

The propaganda, too, catches the same note, and even some of the same statistics Crosfield had worked out for his Kenwood campaign on the desperate need for recreational space, the proportion of applications for playing fields local authorities were rejecting, and the way this side of popular need had been ignored for more than a century in favour of housing, production and transport.

One can also attribute to Crosfield the emphasis on health and welfare, rather than industrial or, still more, military needs. This enabled the Association to assemble a good deal of support from the Labour Party. Ramsay Macdonald was one of its most prominent supporters. So were Snowden, Clynes, and even Sidney Webb. Several notable women of the day were included – Nancy Astor, the Duchess of Atholl. Leading Liberals – Lloyd George himself, Sir John Simon, and Archibald Sinclair – also ranged themselves with the new pressure group.

The Association was designed to exert pressure both centrally – on the Ministry of Health and the Board of Education – and, through its county branches, on local authorities; and this was perhaps its most important role. It also brought in all the governing bodies and organisers of the main sports, nationally and locally. It prepared guidance on minimum standards and areas for tennis, bowling, and pitches for the main team games. But it aimed also at being able to make grants in support of local and national effort.

From the first it was spectacularly successful. Donations of both money and land came pouring in, and many schemes which earlier would have been set aside by cash-conscious local authorities were put into effect. In its first twenty months of life it spent or induced the expenditure of more than one and a half millions. It incidentally provided a useful, non-controversial, and popular occupation for King George V's second son, the Duke of York, who became its first and enthusiastic President. The reputation he gained as a friend of youth and the open air contributed a great deal to his ready acceptance as his elder brother's successor and the resolution of the damaging Abdication Crisis.

Crosfield soldiered on as chairman of the National Playing Fields Association until he was nearly seventy, with the ever-faithful and well-informed Lawrence Chubb always at his side as General Secretary. In 1929 a GBE was added to Crosfield's baronetcy, and in the following year Chubb was knighted – the first professional environmentalist to be so honoured.

These years of achievement and the public success they brought no doubt brought some private happiness too. He frequently travelled to Greece, where his old friend Venizelos was again Prime Minister, and together, in 1934, they visited Crete to inspect the discoveries of Sir Arthur Evans, with whom they celebrated at the Villa Ariadne. At home the pre-Wimbledon tennis parties at 'Witanhurst' were as brilliant as ever. He had now become the close friend of the Duke of York and his wife, who were often seen there. One picture taken at 'Witanhurst' during these years shows three reigning sovereigns and several other royal personages ranged round Arthur and Domini.

But the bitterness and emptiness of his domestic life grew sharper and deeper. Domini's long-standing affair with Colonel Mates was now generally known among his friends, and accepted only in a way such a man must have found humiliating. And on top of this there was another anxiety, namely money.

He had always thought of himself as a wealthy man and had his habitual pleasures – golf, Cannes, occasionally Greece. He was a donor to good causes, though noticeably not on a lavish scale but did not stint private generosity.* He had, and indeed required, a secretary, but otherwise his natural style was modest and affordable. But the vast expense of 'Witanhurst' had made, and was continuing to make, great inroads on his fortune. Domini did not abate her demands in support of her own style of life, even after the affection between them had ended. That star of the Hampstead-Highgate calendar, the tennis party, cost a good deal, and although there were tickets, their proceeds went entirely to Domini's favourite charity, an Islington clinic. She planned to be (and was) Liberal candidate for Islington at the next election. These problems were not made any easier by the economic crisis of 1929–31.

The black moods that had interrupted his schooling and troubled him as a young man began to return

---

* For instance he paid for the education, including the higher education, of the child of the man who had served as his private secretary as an MP, and was killed in the First World War.

and cloud his judgment. Soon after his retirement from the National Playing Fields Association's chairmanship (he continued as Deputy Chairman) and his visit to Greece in 1934, he was introduced by Greek friends to what seemed the possibility of redeeming his fortune. The Rallia mines in Northern Thrace were rich in sulphur and only needed an infusion of capital to become immensely profitable.

His old business instincts were aroused, though without their old shrewdness. So was his muse: he wrote a poem on the subject of sulphur and its properties. It is now lost (at least I fear so) but it was sent to several business friends urging them to enter with him in the promising investment, into which he himself was putting a large sum.

Arthur Crosfield was regarded with affection and trust by his business friends, and it is impossible to think that anything but his judgment was at fault. The Rallia mines failed. He himself lost heavily. So did several of his friends, one of whom was ruined.

Brooding on the misleading of his friends – the gravest offence of all in the business code to which he had been brought up – his black moods became ever more frequent, until Domini became alarmed. In September 1938 they were to take their usual holiday in Cannes and she made an appointment with a distinguished Swiss psychiatrist for a visit by Arthur on the outward journey, needing a short diversion to Geneva. The consultation was held, and Arthur and Domini set out by the night express from Geneva to Cannes. The psychiatrist had recommended he should not be left alone.

They were in separate first-class sleepers, and retired rather late after talking in one of them. During the early morning of 22 September, between Toulon and St Raphael, someone spotted a door swinging open and stopped the train. The door was opposite Arthur's compartment, and he was missing. They found him, dreadfully injured, though not dead, a few hundred yards back along the track, but he was dead when they reached hospital. So ended a life which might have inspired Galsworthy with its weaknesses, its strengths, and its *milieu*.

Ever-loyal, *The Times* displayed the news with great prominence, despite the competing claims of the Munich crisis. There was a memorial service at St Margaret's Westminister at which King George VI and his Queen were represented and the congregation included the whole Liberal leadership and many distinguished industrialists and men of business, besides representatives of the many societies concerned with recreation, sport and open space. The inquest returned a verdict of accidental death, but there were persistent mutterings of suicide. The open door, it was pointed out, was in the corridor, and everything he could possibly have needed during the night was provided in his compartment. Leaving aside 'Witanhurst' his estate was declared at the modest figure of just under £38,000.

Domini lived on in 'Witanhurst' for another two decades, and the tennis parties were still given, though the staff were underpaid and their bedroom lights were restricted to twenty watts. Arthur had intended that after her death it should go to the

129

nation for some public purpose, but that never happened. It is still there, staring over the Heath towards Kenwood, as a monument to a disastrous love.

Taken as a whole, Crosfield's career from his address to the workforce at Warrington in 1892 to his founding chairmanship of the National Playing Fields Association shows him to be one of the greatest pioneers of the movement to rescue and preserve open space from the ever-increasing claims of industrial society. He was one of the first to perceive the threat in its full magnitude. Though not a socialist – far from it – he saw the issues in social terms, drawn from his experience as an industrialist from one of the most polluted parts of the kingdom, and the victims of that industrialism were always at the front of his mind. He had a strong – though a townsman's – affection for the beauties of nature, a passionate belief in the benefits of sport and outdoor recreation, and a measure of nostalgic historicism, but these were rather at the service of his main purpose, than the source of it.

His nervous temperament made him an obsessive and dogged campaigner, fertile in expedients, but above all gifted in attracting support. It is difficult to believe that any but the most attractive personality could have persuaded such men as Mr Whittingham of Harrogate, Mr Wilkinson of Carnforth, Mr Minoprio of Liverpool and Mr Muir MacKean of Paisley to part with such immense sums for an open space hundreds of miles from where they had spent their lives, and for no obvious recognition except one day of glory sharing a platform with the King.

Nor did he seek much recognition for himself from his work as a campaigner. His baronetcy was political, and though his work for the National Playing Fields Association brought him a further decoration it owed a good deal to the personal friendship of the Duke of York and was far from unusual for a life-time of distinguished public service. He created no cult of personality round the causes he took up, and sometimes showed an almost reckless unselfishness.

The struggle for Kenwood shows him at his best as an honourable and undaunted man. Previous major additions to the Heath had attracted at least some government contribution: but in the post-war world of the early 1920's he had to persist alone. But for this persistence, Hampstead Heath would have lost the great sweep that makes it unique, and Lord Iveagh would never have had the opportunity of acquiring the house and Kenwood's last seventy-four acres for the public as the home for the magnificent collection that commemorates his name.

Appendix

The Iveagh Bequest (Kenwood) Act 1929*

This is for those readers who wish to pursue the potent ghost of the first Earl of Iveagh through the legal labyrinth ('divers provisions and dispositions' as the Act calls them) he left behind on the subject of Kenwood. Throughout the journey it is important to remember that nothing Lord Iveagh did, or that the Act says, applied to anything except the property he bought in 1925 and the collection of pictures he already possessed. It does not in any way apply to the South Wood, the ponds, or an area to the north of them, which are easily thought of as 'Kenwood' but

---

* 19 & 20 Geo.5.Ch.lxix 10 May 1929. This private Act of Parliament consists of a Preamble, eight Sections and a Schedule which recites the full text of a Deed of Agreement between all the parties concerned and gives effect to it as law. This Schedule, in turn, contains a Preamble, reciting various relevant documents showing Lord Iveagh's intentions and a scheme of arrangement in eleven long clauses. In what follows references to the Act itself are preceded by the word 'Act', and those to the Deed in the Schedule by 'D'.

had been bought (mainly with municipal money) by the Crosfield campaign of 1924.

Despite all the complexities and changes of detail with which Lord Iveagh decided to surround his intentions, they were perfectly clear from the first, and throughout. He could have conferred land, house and collection on the LCC, subject to certain trusts expressing his wishes; or he could have conferred them on trustees appointed by him and his heirs. But he did neither of these things. He wished and perhaps had promised, that the land would finish up as an addition to Hampstead Heath under the control of the LCC, and the house remain as a picture gallery open to the public for exhibition of his collection, under the control of himself and his family after him. This was why, before buying the freehold and imposing trusts on it, he had taken out the lease for ten years in his own name that caused so much trouble. Financial and tax reasons may also have played a part in this complication.

Unfortunately this idea, comprehensible though it is, posed legal and administrative problems for those who had to carry it out, or were affected by it; and the way his legal advisers had expressed it made other lawyers unhappy. So an Act of Parliament was required, not to substitute something else for Lord Iveagh's clear intentions, but to make them effective, and to conform with the practice of the LCC, who always liked new responsibilities to be backed by statutory authority.

When Lord Iveagh financed trustees to buy the freehold of the house and the seventy-four acres one rood and two perches round and under it he imposed in the purchase document this trust as regards the land:

> To hold . . . the land as an open space for the benefit of the public for ever by way of addition to or extension of Hampstead Heath . . .

and as regards the house:

> for such purposes for the benefit of the public as may from time to time be determined by the trustees for the time being . . . (D Preamble p 7)

and not later than January 1935, or sooner if the trustees so decided, they should hand over both house and land to the London County Council (or any successor authority in charge of Hampstead Heath) to be

> for ever . . . subject to the like purposes in all respects . . . as may for the time being or from time to time be applicable to Hampstead Heath . . .

with the additional trust that as regarded the house it should go on being used in accordance with any decisions the trustees had reached on that point. (D Preamble p 8)

It is clear that the purpose of the house which the trustees should decide, though not specified in the purchase document, was soon thought of by Lord

Iveagh as the home for his pictures. He proceeded a little later to point up this by altering his own will, which he duly did on 9 December 1926. There was some later doubt whether he could unilaterally alter existing trusts in this way, and one of the purposes of the Act of Parliament was to get rid of this shadow.

He altered his will by means of a codicil which made his wishes in respect of the house being used as a picture gallery absolutely clear, and left to his will trustees (not quite the same people as the trustees who owned the freehold of house and land already):

(1) The lease lasting until 1935, which was in his own name, and
(2) An endowment of £50,000 for his proposed gallery and the pictures.

(D Preamble pp 9–10)

The point of doing it in this way, and giving the collection of pictures and the lease of the house to a different body from that owning the freehold of the land, was no doubt to strengthen his intended family hold over the picture collection for ever. This is emphasised by his provision, in the same amendment to his will, that if the collection *ever* ceased to be exhibited to the public in Kenwood it should thereupon go back to his residual estate. (D Preamble p 11)

The Earl of Iveagh is also recorded in the Deed (Clauses 3(6) (c) and 3(7) (c)) as having expressed two 'wishes' about the style of managment he wished to preserve in the house and the surrounding land respectively. But he neither incorporated them in a formal document, nor gave them the status of trusts. Nor does the Deed or the Act impose them on anyone as legal obligations (indeed they are careful to say so), though they express the hope that they will be respected. The 'wish' in respect of the house was:

> 'that the said mansion house and its contents should be preserved as a fine example of the artistic home of a gentleman of the eighteenth century'.

and that in respect of the surrounding land:

> 'that the atmosphere of a gentleman's private park should be preserved'.

Having done all this Lord Iveagh died on 7 October 1927.

§

Lord Iveagh's intentions to have different regimes for the house/collection on the one hand and the land on the other were reasonably clear, but apart from the technical legal doubt hanging over the way he had expressed himself, all those who had to carry out his intention were faced with practical difficulties and unreasonable problems:

> *Lord Iveagh's heirs*, some of whom were also Kenwood Trustees, were perhaps least affected

136

but they found their inheritance diminished not only by a liability to complete the transformation of the house into a picture gallery, but to maintain it and the surrounding land for a period which might last as long as eight years.

The London County Council found that at any time during the next eight years they could be called upon by the Kenwood Trustees, at only six months notice, to take over full responsibility for the house and the land, though not for what went on in the house or for the collection it contained.

The Kenwood Trustees faced the worst problems. Even in those days the yield of their endowment would not be enough (it was £1,500 a year) even to safeguard their precious collection or provide lighting and heating, cleaning, and – worst of all – insurance. The employment of an adequate curator, the cost of even minimal conservation and repairs, the preparation of a catalogue, would be out of the question. They were given no power specifically to charge for admission or to make enforceable rules for visitors. They could not borrow, for they had no security. If they got rid of some (but far from all) of these difficulties by handing their title to land and house over to the LCC, and if the LCC accepted, they still had the responsibility for the collection and the exhibition of it, with little to sustain it, and finding every inch of ground outside their walls controlled by someone else.

It is clear that within a very short time after Lord Iveagh's death urgent discussions began to resolve these difficulties. The first result of them must have been the handover of land and house by the Kenwood trustees to the LCC (18 July 1928). The six months notice required must have been given not later than January 1928, and the decision to give it even earlier. By April 1929, only eighteen months after Lord Iveagh's death, the immense and complicated Deed which forms the marrow of the Kenwood Act had been worked out and signed. What was more the way for a Private Act of Parliament must have been booked, for it passed through all its stages in both Houses and received Royal Assent less than four weeks after the Deed on which it was based was signed.

§

Taking the Act as a whole, including the essential Scheduled Deed, the following was the result:

(1) All the legal doubt about the effectiveness of Lord Iveagh's various provisions (including the validity of the original trusts on the ground that he had reserved a beneficial*

* This was one of the most troublesome of all the loose ends Iveagh had left. If he had a beneficial interest (through his lease) when the freehold was bought he could not create valid charitable trusts on it, and the whole basis of his scheme was flawed.

138

interest by the lease he already owned) were removed (D Cl 1);

(2) The troublesome lease was abolished (Act S 4(1));

(3) The house, and the seventy-four acres, became the freehold property of the LCC, subject to all the trusts imposed on them (Act S 4 (1) and Schedule);

(4) The collection of pictures became the property of the LCC, together with the trusts attaching to them (Act S 4 (1) and Schedule);

But

(5) Effective control of the house and the collection was given to the Guinness Family by creating a body of six 'Administrative Trustees' of whom four were nominees of the Guinness Family. The other two were a representative of the LCC and the Director of the National Gallery *ex officio* (D Cl 5);

(6) The powers of the 'Administrative Trustees' were carefully spelt out to make them a governing body. They could make and enforce regulations for visitors provided the Home Office approved them (Act S 5(1) and (2)) and remove misbehaving members of the public; charge for entry on two days a week;

employ staff 'and if deemed desirable a curator', and have complete control of the income from Lord Iveagh's endowment (D Cl 8(1) and Cl 10);

(7) The Administrative Trustees had equally specific duties. They had to maintain the house, exhibit the collection, and pay all outgoings on both. They had to insure the house (insurance of the pictures was optional). And they had to observe Lord Iveagh's trusts and respect his wish that the house should be kept as 'a fine example of the artistic home of a gentleman of the eighteenth century' (D Cl 7 and 9).

It was also enacted (D Cl 7(a)) that the house (*not* the land or the picture collection) 'shall henceforth be known as 'The Iveagh Bequest''.

Since the LCC was given absolute control of the seventy-four acres of land under these arrangements, it was required to allow access to the house across the land. So far as the public was concerned this access was restricted to the hours the house was open, but as regarded the Administrative Trustees, their agents servants, workmen and anyone else they authorised, at all times, by day or night with or without horses and motor or other vehicles (D Cl 7).

§

This ingenious compromise had one fatal weakness.

It did not provide an adequate income for the upkeep of the house and collection. The trustees were left to manage on the income from their endowment and whatever they could raise by appealing to the public and charging on two days a week. The LCC, far from being empowered to help them, was almost forbidden to do so. Luckily they were given an escape hatch. By Clause 11 of the Deed they were allowed – if they decided they could not carry on – to offer all their powers and responsibilities, and their endowment, to the LCC. If the LCC accepted, the existing body of trustees would go out of existence, and the LCC would succeed them with precisely the same powers and responsibilities. That was what happened in 1949.

The LCC could have refused. If that had happened, the collection and the endowment would have reverted to the Guinness Family, but the house would have gone in any case to the LCC,

> upon trust either to use the same . . . for any purpose for which the same are . . . capable of being used in connection with the said lands . . . under the trusts . . . or upon trust to use the same for the purpose of a public library or museum . . .

What public authority could have refused some of the greatest pictures in the world for nothing? They accepted.

§

141

Appendix

The Iveagh Bequest Act is still the law of the land, and the many trusts it created or validated still preserve their ghostly existence. Even today it is certain that you cannot, on most of the seventy-four acres one rood and two perches, play 'cricket, football, hockey, golf, baseball, real tennis, lawn tennis, badminton, croquet, bowls, or any other game usually or properly played by a team' or, throughout the area, 'alter or interfere with existing contours'. Nor can the house now be used for any other purpose than that of exhibiting Lord Iveagh's pictures and commemorating his name. But there is no commemoration of Crosfield.

Note On Sources

I. *Original Material*

Papers of the Earl of Mansfield at Scone Palace (NRA (S) 0776) (referred to in footnotes as 'M' with Box or Bundle number and date of item).

Warrington Public Library. Crosfield Collection.

Information Library of Messrs Unilever plc. Papers of the First Viscount Leverhulme.

British Library, BL Add. MS. 62112. Autobiographical MS of Humphry Repton.

London Borough of Camden, Swiss Cottage Local History Collection. Records of the Heath Protection Society.

Greater London Record Office. Records of the London County Council.

Crosfield, Sir Arthur:
Reminiscences of Kenwood and the Northern Heights (1925) reprinted from *Country Life.*
A Pilgrimage of Empire (1916).

Murray's *Handbook of Warrington* (1870).

Records of the National Playing Fields' Association.

Hansard.

The Times.

The Illustrated London News.

Country Life.

Hampstead and Highgate Express.

Highgate Literary and Scientific Institution. Local History Collection.

Information from Miss Kathleen Smith, former private secretary to Lady Crosfield.

Information from Sir Nicholas Goodison.

II. *Selected Secondary Works*

Bryant, Julius, *The Iveagh Bequest Kenwood* (English Heritage 1990)

Campbell, Lord, *Lives of the Lord Chief Justices* (1849)

Crosfield, John Fothergill, *The Crosfield Family*. Revised Edition (Cambridge 1990)

Guinness, Michele, *the Guinness Legend* (1989)

Heward, E, *Lord Mansfield* (1979)

Ikin, C W, *How the Heath was Saved* (1971)

Musson, A E, *Enterprise in Soap and Chemicals: The Crosfields of Warrington* (Manchester 1965)

Simon, Jacob, *Humphry Repton at Kenwood (Camden History Review* 1984)

Stroud, Dorothy, *Humphry Repton* 1962

Summerson, Sir John, *The Iveagh Bequest Kenwood* (English Heritage 1988)

144

Thompson, F W L, *Hampstead, the Making of a Borough* (1974)

Victorian County History vol vi Middlesex (Manor of Hornsey)

§

Somewhere, perhaps, what must have been the voluminous records of the Kenwood Preservation Council still survive, but my enquiries have failed to trace any except the documents kindly made available to me by Sir Nicholas Goodison. Even copies of its appeals are rare items, as are its Interim (1923) and Final (1925) Reports.

Index

146

Index

Index

Index

Index